How the Ideals of America's Founders
Lead Us to Purposeful Living

ROGER FORTIN

Distinguished Service
Professor of History
Xavier University

Cincinnati Book Publishing

Cincinnati, Ohio

Cincinnati Book Publishing
Cincinnati, Ohio

Anthony W. Brunsman, President and CEO
Sue Ann Painter, Executive editor
Kara Thompson, Associate editor
Cover design by Jonathan Witte

Dr. Fortin portrait by Gregory Rust

ISBN   978-1-7327493-5-1

eBook ISBN   978-1-7327493-6-8

Library of Congress Control Number: 2019939168

Printed in the United States of America
First Edition, 2019

To purchase additional copies online, visit www.cincybooks.com.
Discounts available on quantity orders. Email: info@cincybooks.com or
call 513-382-4315.

Dedication

To all my former students for their inspiration.

Contents

FOREWORD

Roger Fortin has explored the promise of American life with family, friends, and, above all, his many students for over half a century. I know of no one who has taken more pleasure in teaching than Roger. Although he spent much of his prodigious talent and energy in administrative work, Roger never strayed far from the classroom. His love of teaching, respect for learning, and care for students guided everything he did, in and out of the classroom. Personally, I find teaching, for all its rewards, a struggle. When colleagues offer the usual "have fun in class today," I am incredulous. It's work, wonderful, rewarding work, but work nonetheless, and hard work at that. Fun has little to do with it for me. But I never doubted that Roger genuinely enjoyed his time in the classroom and his students are the better for his efforts.

We have here, then, Roger Fortin's latest gift to his students, written in a joyful, hopeful, and inspirational tone. Fortin traces the promise of American life back to the founding generation. In his view, the Founders hoped to make it possible for Americans to live as deeply and fully as possible by providing a foundation for the security and happy enjoyment of life and liberty for each individual. Without ignoring the prejudices of the founding generation and the flaws in what they built, Fortin celebrates their accomplishment and finds inspiration in their lasting ideals. He places those ideals at the center of what he and others call the American dream, a recurring set of aspirations that shape the hopes of generation after generation.

But were it not for the thirty-five years of fond friendship that Roger and I have enjoyed, I might seem a strange choice to author a foreword to this book. To use a word Roger has applied to my disposition, my view of the founding generation is somewhat more morose. "Having seen human nature on display in the marketplace, the courtroom, the legislative chamber, and in every secret path and alleyway where wealth and power are courted," wrote the distinguished historian Richard Hofstadter of the Founders, "they felt they knew it in all its frailty." In Hofstadter's view, they based the Constitution on the philosophy of Thomas Hobbes and the theology of Jean Calvin, a war of all against all, unfolding among depraved humans. "They did not believe in man," Hofstadter concluded, "but they did believe in the power of a good constitution to control him." Still a noble accomplishment, if not entirely a democratic one, and one being tested, yet again, as I write.[1]

So despite my gloomy view, I know we need Fortin's hopeful and cogent voice in these troubled times, when divisions of class, race, gender, ethnicity, and partisanship threaten our tattered republic. As Fortin points out, Americans have often returned to the Founders for guidance when our republican commitments to legal procedures, civil liberties, and political equality have been under attack. We would do well at this juncture to consider the Founders' accomplishments, and the efforts of subsequent generations to protect, amend, and improve on those accomplishments. We are unlikely to find our better selves by ignoring their work.

Fortin's emphasis on the pursuit of happiness, moreover, leads us back to the time before the Constitution, to the Declaration of Independence. The decade-long, disillusioning "times that try men's souls," in Thomas Paine's famous phrase, led the Founders to distrust the virtue of the people. In the Constitution, they hedged the more hopeful bets they had made in 1776. In the Declaration, as the political scientist Danielle Allen argues, the Founders recognized that individual happiness depended on "egalitarian access to the instrument of government." Thomas Jefferson's carefully crafted text linked the individual goal of "life, liberty, and the pursuit of happiness" to the collective effort "to secure those rights" through the political process. Jefferson's analysis of certain "self-evident truths," Allen writes, "leads us from the individual to the community—from our separate and equal rights to what we can achieve only together." Here is Fortin's "one for all and all for one." [2]

Perhaps today we are finally paying attention to the vast and grotesque inequality in our society. The election of Donald Trump may well be one product of the recognition that the American dream is dead for too many. But the past two years have only further dampened hope in that dream. It is time to reengage the vision of Abraham Lincoln, who himself engaged and updated the vision of the Founders. Lincoln embraced the Declaration of Independence, rather than the Constitution, as the true American charter. The principles of the Declaration, Lincoln told the American people, should be understood as collective duties rather than individual rights, "constantly looked to, constantly labored for, and even though never perfectly attained, constantly approximated." Lincoln understood the egalitarian propositions of the Declaration not as established conditions to be protected by limited government but as positive goals for an active government. The point, after all, is to make the dream a reality. Roger Fortin's fine study can help us do that. [3]

John D. Fairfield

Professor of History, Xavier University

Preface

In my fifty-plus years of teaching, the Founding Fathers' ideals and America's mission figured prominently in all my classes. They proved helpful to me and to my students. Since the nation's founding Americans have latched on them, encouraging refinement of those qualities that characterize individuals at their finest. It is this generation's responsibility to continue to build upon this heritage, caring about how we live our lives and how we help others.

I am indebted to Dr. John Fairfield, Professor of History and long-time friend, for his careful analysis of the manuscript and valuable suggestions and to Sue Ann Painter, Executive Editor, Cincinnati Book Publishing, for her editing and recommendations. I am also grateful to my Xavier colleagues, namely Darleen Frickman for her assistance in preparing the manuscript for publication; Gregory Rust, Director for Photography, Marketing, and Communication for providing the portrait photograph; Brian Maley, Director of Alumni Relations, for reaching out to graduates on my behalf; and Gary Massa, Vice President for University Relations, for his support. Lastly, I would also like to thank my faculty colleagues for their friendship, creativity, and commitment to academic excellence.

INTRODUCTION

In the spring of 1925, the students' newspaper at Cincinnati's St. Xavier College, which became Xavier University in 1930, sponsored a contest to find an appropriate nickname for the school's athletic teams. In the fall, it announced the name Musketeers as the winner. The Jesuit Francis J. Finn, a faculty member, trustee, and internationally known author of twenty-one books, submitted the name. He thought the motto "one for all and all for one," English translation for "un pour tous et tous pour un," that was attached to the legendary characters in Alexandre Dumas's nineteenth century novel *The Three Musketeers*, ought to reflect the spirit of the teams. Though Dumas's phrase was "all for one and one for all," Fr. Finn thought that each team participant supports the group and all team members pledge to support each individual member, thus "one for all and all for one." The motto also reflects America's mission. "United we stand," Dumas wrote, "divided we fall."

In August 1966, forty-one years after the adoption of the Xavier motto, my wife, Janet, two sons, Thomas and Michael, and I arrived in Cincinnati. A month later I joined the University as an assistant professor in the department of history. After teaching half a century at Xavier, in December 2016 I retired. During my tenure, I was promoted to the rank of professor and then had the honor of being appointed to various administrative positions, including Deanship of Edgecliff College of Xavier University, Academic Vice President, and Provost. These positions and camaraderie with faculty and administrative colleagues proved beneficial to me both personally and professionally. However, my most rewarding position was that of teacher. Though I am the author of numerous scholarly articles and five books, including *Faith and Action: A History of the Catholic*

Archdiocese of Cincinnati, 1821–1996 (2002), *To See Great Wonders: A History of Xavier University, 1831–2006* (2006), and *Fellowship: History of the Cincinnati Irish* (2018), there was no greater satisfaction than engaging and interacting with students.

Today, the Fortin family, consisting of thirty-two members, including six children, fourteen grandchildren, four step-grandchildren, and two step-great grandchildren, are proud to be members of the Xavier family. All six living children are graduates of the University. Xavier is in our blood, so to speak.

It has been said that every book is a journey. My years at Xavier have proven to be a pleasant and rewarding experience. I hope that my relationship and interaction with students proved educational and beneficial to them as well. Significantly, this book affords me the opportunity to elaborate on themes and thoughts that students and I studied and discussed, especially the Founding Fathers' ideals that are central to America's mission and quality of life. Overall, I've learned that while many of my students hoped to secure a meaningful and rewarding career, they also were very much interested in being men and women for others and living a purposeful and fulfilling life. In my judgment, the latter is critically important. Many students and alumni give a few hours per week to help the less fortunate. In my last day teaching in April 2016, I distributed to my students "Personal Reflections on Living a Purposeful Life," a copy of which is in Appendix A. For individual Americans to live life deeply, fully, and meaningfully is not only personally rewarding but enables them to be on more solid ground while caring for others.

CHAPTER ONE
FOUNDING FATHERS' IDEALS
AND AMERICA'S PROMISE

Historically, the concept "one for all and all for one" was conceived in the imagination of sixteenth and seventeenth century Western Europeans who looked to America for individual freedom, liberty, and opportunities. More particularly, New England Puritans, who bravely crossed the Atlantic Ocean to worship God in their own light, built a new community and had a shared sense of purpose. Not only did they have a sense of mission for themselves and their children, but for others as well. Before they set foot on Massachusetts soil in 1630, they declared: "We must delight in each other, make others' condition our own, rejoice together, mourn together, labor and suffer together, always having before our eyes our. . . community in the work, our community as members of the same body." That was their corporate dream: "one for all and all for one."[1]

Benjamin Franklin, Thomas Jefferson, John Adams, and other Founding Fathers, who led the patriot charge for America's independence from England in the 1770s, expanded the concept. Living in a predominantly rural setting, they conceived a society that they hoped would "provide for the security, the quiet, and happy enjoyment of life, liberty, and property" for all. Having a common devotion to those ideals, they marshaled the necessary energy to act on their political imagination.[2]

In late spring 1776 prominent Virginians drafted the Virginia Declaration of Rights, in which they declared that "all men are created equally free and independent, and have certain inherent natural rights, of which they cannot, by any compact, deprive . . . their posterity; among which are the enjoyment of life and liberty, with the means of acquiring and possessing property, and pursuing and obtaining happiness and safety." In July, colonial delegates at the Second Continental Congress in Philadelphia adopted the Declaration of Independence. Franklin, Jefferson, and Adams had been chosen to be on the five-man committee to write the document, which was clearly written by Jefferson with a few minor changes by Adams and Franklin. Jefferson was known to the delegates for the felicity of his pen.[3]

In the Declaration of Independence, the delegates professed the "self-evident" truths that "all Men are created equal, that they are endowed by their Creator with certain unalienable Rights, that among these are Life, Liberty, and the pursuit of Happiness." Few words in American history are more familiar and important than those words. Significantly, the Declaration enshrines the country's basic principles of individual freedom, equality, justice, security, and opportunity for all. In virtually all my courses, such as Formative Years of the Republic, U.S. Intellectual History, and seminars on the American Character and the American Dream, the Founding Fathers' ideals figured prominently. As will be shown later, notwithstanding prejudices, racism, and gender disparity in the 1770s, the Founders viewed their ideals as basic rights, which laid the foundation for America's promise. Their ideals animated the concept "one for all and all for one." Individuals, they thought, should develop themselves as fully as possible, live a purposeful life, and do their part in helping others.

The Founders were visionaries. They had a shared sense of purpose and imagined the new nation holding a special place in history. They preeminently fulfilled the role of makers of the American experiment. Hoping that America would become a model for other countries, they inaugurated a new chapter in the western world. Their writings contain a rich vein of ideas, reflecting the heart of our heritage. As will be shown, each generation of Americans has been guided by the Founders' ideals. In particular, the Declaration of Independence has continuously been a source of inspiration. Through it early political leaders provided an articulate vision of the American promise.[4]

Reflecting and building upon the ideals embodied in the Declaration, various writings, educational essays, and Fourth of July orations in the first twenty years of the new nation discussed those elements needed to establish a just and viable society. It was a time of extraordinary thought. In lucid and imaginative prose the Fourth of July orators, consisting of jurists, clergymen, lawyers, physicians, and retired military officers, monitored the fears, hopes, and dreams of the American people. In the process they expressed what they deemed possible and desirable. "The present critical moment" in history, declared the Congregationalist minister Enos Hitchcock in his Fourth of July oration in Connecticut, "is teeming with the happiness or wretchedness of millions yet unborn." Without succumbing to utopian illusions, the political visionaries viewed themselves as citizens on the threshold of a new age. America was destined to become, argued James Madison of Virginia and a principal drafter of the U.S. Constitution, "the workshop of liberty" in the world.[5]

As architects of the new nation, the Founders demonstrated a deep sense of a righteous and virtuous nation being formed, one that would serve and care for everyone. Promoting growth in commerce and manufacturing, many of them believed that egotism and greed discouraged individuals from pursuing the larger social good, thereby threatening America's ideals. They argued that personal pleasure had to be tempered by virtue. According to John Adams, who was the leading constitutional thinker and one of the most learned statesmen of his day, passion and appetite are as much a part of man as reason and moral sense. "Wherever men, women, or children, are to be found, whether they be old or young, rich or poor, high or low, wise or foolish, ignorant or learned," he argued, "every individual is seen to be strongly actuated by a desire to be seen, heard, talked of, approved and respected by the people about him."[6]

As the new Constitution of the United States was being ratified in the late 1780s, Adams further argued that "the insatiability of human passions . . . is the foundation of all government. Men are not only ambitious, but their ambition is unbounded; they are not only avaricious, but their avarice is insatiable. The desires of king, gentlemen and common people, —all increase instead of being satisfied by indulgence." Thus, he concluded, "it is necessary to place checks upon them all." The Founders were very much aware that the new nation was as susceptible to human passions and appetites as were individuals.[7]

Yet, how could the newly created republic best protect its citizens against the evils of greed and corruption? Had not all the great republics of the past, like Greece and Rome, succumbed to them? Familiar with the writings of Aristotle and contemporary European thinkers like John Locke, David Hume, and Adam Smith, the Founding Fathers understood that human desire could never be permanently satisfied and had to have limits. They argued that desire without restrictions was problematic. "Few men," George Washington observed, "have virtue to withstand the highest bidder."[8]

While acknowledging that man was imperfect, some Founders nevertheless agreed with Thomas Jefferson that man "was endowed with a sense of right and wrong. . . . This sense is as much a part of his nature as the sense of hearing, seeing, feeling; it is the true foundation of morality. . . . The moral sense, or conscience," he continued, "is as much a part of man as his leg or arm. . . [and] may be strengthened by exercise, as may any particular limb of the body."[9]

Though Adams and Jefferson had different political affiliations and differed on the nature of man, the former believing that man was basically a sinner and Jefferson that man was basically good, they both agreed that education would go a long way to help man lead a more righteous life. Following their presidencies, 1797-1801 and 1801-1809 respectively, they became good friends and had a rich correspondence, much of which dealt with America's ideals and promise. They both died on the same day, July 4, 1826, the fiftieth anniversary of the Declaration of Independence.

Through the Constitution of the United States, which was adopted in 1789, the Founders established a nation of laws and a political system with checks and balances largely to prevent the abuse of power. Montesquieu, the eighteenth-century French political philosopher who influenced them and was especially concerned over authoritarianism and powerful rulers, warned that a free society must guard against "negligence, mistakes, . . . dangerous examples, [and] the seeds of corruption." Enslavement by tyranny was of great concern during the American Revolution. A consequence of the war for independence was the power that people wanted to exercise over themselves.[10]

A free people, the Founding Fathers thought, should be governed by law and not by the impulses of individuals. The Constitution with its safeguards has served as a framework of American political and economic life for approximately 230 years. The Founders saw civic virtue as necessary to maintain liberty as well as acting selflessly for the common good. For them, individual interest and the greater good, private and public happiness, could and should exist side by side.[11]

But for individualism and social responsibility to coexist, they thought, depended heavily on formal education. Early American leaders hoped to provide a liberal arts education and implant in the minds of young people the principles of virtue and liberty that would enable them to act as independent human beings, making it possible for them to fulfill their dreams and live fuller lives. In their wisdom, they believed education was essential for individuals to better themselves. The Founders hoped, as did James Madison, that when people "have the means of knowledge" they "adopt right political sentiments" and attend to the needs of others. They insisted that a free society cannot survive without quality education.[12]

Assuming, then, that a person is educable and that the manners of a free people depend greatly upon knowledge, most American leaders in the formative years of the new nation proposed that learning be generously encouraged. In independent America, stressed the Massachusetts politician, Thomas Dawes, in his keynote address at the Fourth of July celebration in Boston's historic Faneuil Hall in 1787, the "arts and sciences" should "spread far and wide." On the same day in New Haven, Connecticut, the lawyer David Daggett, who later became prominent in national politics, also urged the state legislature to support the spread of knowledge to "induce" individuals "to think and act for themselves." The Founding Fathers hoped that the new nation would soon produce, in addition to more scientists and mechanics, her share of poets, critics, and historians.[13]

Believing that authority should reside in the people, they were out to prove to themselves and to the world that free individuals could govern successfully. But the success of the experiment, they thought, clearly rested on the quality of education, independent individual thinking, and on free and open dissemination of knowledge and criticism. "When I speak of a diffusion of knowledge," explained the Massachusetts lexicographer Noah Webster, (and he may very well have been expressing the sentiments of most of his educational colleagues), "I do not mean merely a knowledge of spelling books and the New Testament." Individuals in a free society need an "acquaintance with ethics and with the general principles of law, commerce, money, and government." The Founders cared about the character of individuals, how they live their lives.[14]

Having then, a high opinion of human capabilities, prominent speakers on politics and education asserted that the whole society stood to profit by an investment in education. The Connecticut jurist, Simeon Baldwin, captured the founding generation's sense of the potential power of an educated citizenry in his 1788 Independence Day address, saying that the degree of oppression in society "will ever be in proportion to the knowledge and refinement of the people." Where education is confined to a few people, wrote the Philadelphia statesman Benjamin Rush in his *Plan for the Establishment of Public Schools*, "we always find monarchy, aristocracy, or slavery." Because in America the people fill the branches of government, education "is the rock" on which America must build her "political salvation."[15]

For this reason, Thomas Jefferson, writing from Paris in the summer of 1786, urged his friend and former mentor George Wythe of Virginia to join him in "a crusade against ignorance. . . . The tax which would be paid to promote the education of the common people," he argued, "is not more than the thousandth part of what will be paid to kings . . . and nobles who will rise among us if we leave the people in ignorance." During the next half century America became the first country to publicly fund mass general education. Significantly, it should be noted that what Jefferson and others proposed was an education that would enable individuals to develop their critical and moral faculties as fully as possible. For the Founding Fathers, then, the most practical education is a liberal education that helps develop an individual's critical and moral faculties.[16]

Adams, Jefferson, and Madison, who would become our country's second, third, and fourth Presidents of the United States respectively, were committed to the concept of a republic. They envisioned a society of free and self-sufficient individuals, a republic of independent producers. What they did not want was a hereditary aristocracy, people who had no other qualification for office than having been born into a privileged family. Rather, most of them espoused a natural aristocracy, people of demonstrated talent and virtue who earned the right to represent the people. "I agree with you," Jefferson wrote to Adams, "that there is a natural aristocracy among men. The grounds of this are virtue and talents."[17]

America's early political leaders generally attained their stature, as Benjamin Franklin did, through merit. For the Founders, merit was largely attained through education, experience, and virtue. Virtue was especially important. According to the historian Jon Meacham, Jefferson's contemporary biographer, Jefferson firmly believed that "the will of an educated, enlightened majority should prevail." They, in turn, Madison thought, will "select men of virtue and wisdom."[18]

When the Founders set out to fashion society in such a way as to make it possible for individuals to pursue their individual dreams, there were glaring paradoxes in the American situation. While the Declaration of Independence symbolized the dignity and worth of the individual, there was the obvious anomaly of America's dedication both to the principles of the Declaration of Independence and to the institution of slavery. Though primarily founded on the principles of liberty and equality, the newly born country was approximately half free. Three prominent Founders from Virginia, namely George Washington, Thomas Jefferson, and James Madison, owned hundreds of slaves.

Early American leaders were a mirror of their culture. At the time of the Declaration of Independence enslaved Americans, women, and Native Americans were not viewed as equals to white men. The Founders were composed of that same mesh of good and evil that people are generally made of. During the nineteenth century millions of Native Americans were removed from their land, slaves from Africa continued to be imported and bred, and women were legally subordinated to men. The professed "self-evident" truths that all individuals "are endowed by their Creator with certain unalienable Rights, that among these are Life, Liberty, and the pursuit of Happiness," were not so self-evident. They applied more to a minority of the population than to everyone.

Notwithstanding the Founders' flaws and later generations' prejudices, their ideals have proven over time to be more energizing. They are at the core of America's mission. In response to the U.S. Supreme Court Dred Scott decision in 1857, which said that a black person, whose ancestors were slaves, was not an American citizen and could not sue in a federal court, the nineteenth-century former slave and African American leader Frederick Douglass wrote: "I know of no soil better adapted to the growth of reform than the American soil. I know of no country where the conditions for . . . the development of right ideas of liberty and humanity, are more favorable than here in the United States."

In the late 1800s, when the country moved from a rural-agrarian to an industrial-urban society and became a leading industrial power in the world, there was much to celebrate. However, there was also much to mend. Americans lived through a period of racial, ethnic, labor, and urban violence. Many new immigrants, ghetto dwellers, poor rural folks, black people, women, and American Indians could barely make a living, never mind trying to pursue their dreams. Nevertheless, success was real for many people. It certainly proved true for some immigrants. The young country offered immigrants, largely from Ireland and Germany, freedom to dream, develop a skill or trade, work hard, and achieve as much as they could. Of course, not all immigrants upon their arrival to America succeeded. Many were faced with financial hardships and social isolation through prejudices and exclusions.

Indeed, while America is a story of fulfillment and success for many people, it is also a story of omissions. In every generation there has been a deviation from the ideals of life, liberty, and the pursuit of happiness for all. Notwithstanding the fact that in each generation there have been cracks in the American promise, what has been strong throughout our history is the notion that our nation's unique ideals of freedom, equality, justice, and opportunity for all are the most conducive to progress.

What each generation has had in common is the firm belief in the Founders' ideals, which are the core, the essence of America's identity. They have been a great force in our history. Each generation has carried them forward. Through such moments as the Women's Rights Convention in 1848, President Abraham Lincoln's Gettysburg Address in 1863, and Martin Luther King, Jr.'s "I Have a Dream" speech a century later, subsequent generations of Americans expanded the ideals embodied in the Declaration of Independence, the Bill of Rights, and the U.S. Constitution. Over time women, blacks, and minorities achieved rights incrementally. For example, blacks, women, and gays at the end of World War II were less confident about attaining their dreams than many of their descendants over half a century later. The struggles over civil rights, women's rights, and gay rights testify to the timeless value of our nation's ideals as they relate to individual rights.

Each generation of Americans has measured its success against the Founding Fathers' ideals. Inextricably bound to the principles in the Declaration of Independence, the concept "one for all and all for one," which is at the heart of the American promise, is a moral imperative, a moral standard to which we should strive. In all my classes, students and I discussed the importance, both personally and collectively, of living true to America's values. As is often true in teaching, by discussing the Founders' ideals and values they were reinforced in me.

"All for one and one for all," *The Three Musketeers,*

Alexandre Dumas

CHAPTER TWO
THE AMERICAN DREAM

In their recurring optimism about the future, each generation of Americans expressed faith in the Founding Fathers' ideals of freedom, equality, and opportunity for every citizen. Over time, this optimism became identified with the concept of the American Dream. What precisely have Americans meant by it? What are its defining features? It's a term that was and is often used broadly and has meant different things to different people. We live in a country made up of dreams. And at a time when the world is so interconnected, the Dream has no national boundaries. It extends beyond the United States.

The American Dream has been alluded to by scores of individuals, ranging from politicians, business leaders, academicians, and news commentators to folks in various walks of life. To some people the concept is success measured by money, power, and fame. To others the term may connote freedom, equality, opportunity, free enterprise, upward mobility, owning a home, or good job, among others. It has been used in different settings. When the Cincinnati Reds professional baseball team won the National League Central Division in 2010, the headline in the *Cincinnati Enquirer* read in bold letters: GREAT AMERICAN DREAM COMES TRUE. As Jim Cullen points out in *The American Dream* (2003), the Dream is "an idea that seems to envelop us as unmistakably as the air we breathe."[1]

There are reputable books written on the American Dream. The first known scholar to use the term was Walter Lippmann in his book, *Drift and Mastery*, published in 1914. He used it only once. An intellectual and political commentator, Lippmann argued that the American Dream "may be summed up . . . in the statement that the undisciplined man is the salt of the earth." That statement affirmed his "belief in the virtues of the spontaneous, enterprising, . . . and unsocialized man." Like the muckrakers of his day, who identified scores of economic and social injustices in society, Lippmann hoped America could be restored so that "each man could again be left to his own will," that every individual would be able to affirm his individuality as much as possible. Concerned over the significant disparity of income and the problems that ordinary people faced in America in the early 1900s, he further argued that creating "a minimum standard of life below which no human being can fall is the most elementary duty of [our] democratic state."[2]

Lippmann thought as did Herbert Croly in his book *The Promise of American Life*, published five years earlier in 1909, a book that President Theodore Roosevelt at the time very much admired. Americans "can no longer treat life as something that has trickled down to us," Croly wrote. "We have to deal with it deliberately, devise its social organization." Both Lippmann and Croly underscored the need to enact reforms in society to realize the promise of American life. "Americans have always had," Croly maintained, "the liveliest and completed faith in the process of individual and social improvement," and for America to continue to be the land of promise, it must remain true to its ideals. Seeking to revitalize the Founding Fathers' ideals, Presidents Theodore Roosevelt and Woodrow Wilson, a Republican and Democrat respectively, favored legislation to promote fair competition and prevent abuses. They wanted the federal government to play a vital role in regulating markets to protect public health and safety.[3]

Notwithstanding Lippmann's first use of the term American Dream, it has long been acknowledged by the historical community that the Pulitzer Prize writer and historian, James Truslow Adams, popularized it in his 1931 book, *The Epic of America*. He used it over thirty times. Though the term did not become part of the American vernacular until then, the concept, Adams argued, began "to take form in the hearts of men" in the early 1600s in the colonial settlements of Jamestown, Plymouth, and Boston. He maintained that the American Dream was a vital force from the start. "The economic motive," he wrote, "was unquestionably powerful, often dominant, in the minds of those who [left Europe and] took part in the great migration" to America. But "mixed" with the economic motive, Adams argued, was "the hope of a better and a freer life, a life in which a man might think as he would and develop as he willed."[4]

From the beginning America was seen by many as the "promised land." According to Adams the seventeenth- and eighteenth-century immigrants "had glimpsed the American dream." English, Scotch, Irish, and Germans came to America "to find security and self-expression. They came with a new dynamic hope of rising and growing, of hewing out for themselves a life . . . not only of economic prosperity but of social and self-esteem." Consistently throughout *The Epic of America* he argued that the dream arose reflected the feelings "of the common mass of men."[5]

Significantly, Adams wrote much about the struggle for independence, the Founders' ideals, and Jefferson's leadership as they relate to the Dream and the common man. This is what he noted when he got to the presidency of Andrew Jackson in the 1830s. "At the low end of both the economic and the intellectual scale," Adams wrote, "[the common man's] material needs bulked large. But he also had his idealism. . . . What he asked was what he thought America stood for—opportunity, the chance to grow into something bigger and finer, as bigger and finer appeared to him. [The common man]," Adams continued, "did not envisage America as standing for wealth only; . . .[He] envisaged it as freedom and opportunity for himself and those like him to rise." He noted that from the time independence was won in 1783, every generation for the next century and a half witnessed some expression or movement to affirm the Dream for every American of whatever rank or condition.[6]

Throughout the *Epic,* Adams emphasized that the common man's dream "was a great dream." America's "shrine," he insisted, "has been in the heart of the common man. . . . While the wealthy in the stratified societies of Europe were secure in their status, the poor dared not dream." But, he argued, "[t]hat was not the case for the common man in America." Adams, who had been a successful businessman in a New York brokerage house before he became a historian, believed that the fact that the common man dared to dream "is what . . . made [him] a great figure in the American drama. This is the dominant motif in the American epic."[7]

According to Adams that was the essence of the American Dream. He insisted that the Dream was America's "distinctive and unique gift to mankind. . . . If America has stood for anything unique in the history of the world," he wrote, "it has been for the American dream, the belief in the common man and the insistence upon his having, as far as possible, equal opportunity in every way with the rich one." By every way, he included personally enriching as well as economic opportunities for all Americans.[8]

As the Dream persisted to "strengthen the heart of man," Adams argued, the nineteenth century Romantics Ralph Waldo Emerson and Walt Whitman, who both emphasized the importance of individualism, would remain two of its main prophets. In Adams's judgment, Walt Whitman "caught a vision . . . of the whole of America and of its . . . democratic dreams." Great poetry, Whitman claimed, was always the "result of a national spirit, and not the privilege of a polish'd and select few," and he determined that "without yielding an inch the workingman and the working woman were to be in [his] pages from first to last."[9]

Writing at the beginning of the Great Depression, Adams further argued that "if the dream is to come true, those on top, financially, intellectually, or otherwise, have got to devote themselves to the [betterment of society], . . . and those who are below in the scale have got to strive to rise, not merely economically, but culturally. . . . The very foundation of the American dream of a better and richer life for all is that all, in varying degrees, shall be capable of wanting to share in it." To make "the dream come true," he maintained, Americans "must all work together," namely "one for all and all for one." Adams's *Epic*, like some other works published shortly before and during the Great Depression, awakened Americans to the values of their past. It helped people think about the many challenges that faced the United States as well as the direction in which the country was moving. While Adams saw the need for national planning, he did so to a limit. That is, not at the expense of individual self-development. Though he wanted a more engaged government, he did not want it to be so big as to encroach upon individual rights, liberties, and self-reliance.[10]

Indeed, a basic right of every American is the right to dream. It is America's promise. Individuals are truly free when they are able and active in pursuing their dreams. Moreover, individual pursuits collectively constitute the moral and economic engines that drive this nation forward. The more freedom, equality, and opportunities there are in society, the greater likelihood more people can pursue their goals. Conversely, the less freedom, equality, and fewer opportunities there are, that much smaller is the number of people who engage in that pursuit. There is a direct relationship between the number of individuals who pursue their goals and the health of society. The greater the number of people who can pursue their dream, the healthier is society. The smaller the number, the less healthy is the community.

Though at times confidence in America is shaken, many individuals latch on to the country's principles and the American Dream. The Founders' ideals are an essential part of the glue that holds the nation together. In difficult times, such as during periods of social and economic uncertainty, people question if the American Dream can still be realized. For many individuals the pursuit of the Dream remains elusive. Millions encounter discrimination or have little security and little income. While some argue that the glue is loosening, there are others who express faith in their ability to fulfill their dream.

There is also a certain mystique associated with the pursuit of a dream. As individuals strive toward their goal, whether it is education, career, personal fulfillment, and the like, they are never sure they can attain it. There's always an element of uncertainty. Dreams are not typically easy to achieve. If they were, they would not be dreams. Moreover, at times individuals have inflated expectations. To be sure, however, when an individual has a dream, and that individual is free and has opportunities to pursue it, and works toward the realization of that dream, it is very energizing. When the individual attains it, it is truly fulfilling.

President Ronald Reagan aptly defined the Dream in his 1986 State of the Union Address. "The American dream," he said, "is a song of hope . . . that warms our hearts when the least among us aspire to the greatest things: [such as] to venture a daring enterprise; to unearth new beauty in music, literature, and art; to discover a new universe inside a tiny silicon chip or a single human cell." Reagan's definition is entirely in keeping with America's promise of the possibility of human fulfillment for everyone. Every individual has the right to live, to work, to be oneself, to reasonably attain fulfillment, and to become whatever his talent can potentially enable him to become.[11]

America's promise has always been that individuals willing to learn, work, and play by the rules would have a fair chance to realize their goal. In keeping with the American Dream, individuals generally seek to be left to their own will, to become – as much as possible – masters of their own destiny. Hard-working Americans and enterprising individuals have always been important in the development of the country. But so has been the role of the federal government, such as in providing land grants to railroads in the nineteenth century that made possible the construction of rail lines, employment of thousands of people, and expansion of America; the G. I. Bill, the Servicemen's Readjustment Act of 1944, that provided higher education opportunities for returning World War II veterans; and the construction of interstate highways in the 1950s to improve the nation's infrastructure as well as to stimulate the economy.

AMERICANS' RECURRING HOPEFULNESS ABOUT THE FUTURE

Since the formative years of the new nation many Americans have been influenced by the Founding Fathers' ideals of life, liberty, and the pursuit of happiness and comforted by the belief that they can fulfill their dreams. And a people's attitude about what lies ahead has no small influence on their actions. As the late artist and sociologist, John McHale, pointed out in his treatise, *The Future of the Future* (1969), "[b]y assuming a future, man makes his present endurable, and his past meaningful." A people's belief that they can attain their goals affects their modes of expression, how they live their lives. If their vision of tomorrow is promising, then they are more inclined to make sacrifices and endure hardships in anticipation of the realization of their goals.[12]

Each generation of Americans has served as a nostalgic mirror of the nation's highest ideals and has made repetitive optimistic value judgments about the future. Each has seen America as a land of promise, liberty, and opportunity, which is a difficult expectation to fulfill consistently. The country has had no shortage of individuals preaching the idea of progress, expressing the conviction that individuals can improve themselves and, more generally, the human condition. From the beginning political leaders expressed faith in the educability of man and in the individual's capacity to usher in reforms and enhance the community's quality of life. They argued, as did James Madison, that "[l]earned institutions ought to be favorite objects with every free people."[13]

For over 200 years Americans have been acting out of a future-oriented pattern of social redemption. America has had four significant transformative periods in its history: 1603-1815, 1815-1945, 1945-1990s, and 1990s to the present. Each transformative period celebrated the latest development in mechanics and technology and witnessed a profound alteration in which individual and collective behavior and social values and institutions changed dramatically. Moreover, during each transition there was some modification of old jobs as well as new ones created.

In 1831 Timothy Walker, an Irish attorney from Cincinnati,

wrote an essay on "Defense of Mechanical Philosophy" in the *North American Review*. It was a critical rejoinder to the Scottish philosopher Thomas Carlyle's anti-mechanical essay, "Signs of the Times," published two years earlier in the *Edinburgh Review*. Walker argued that machines were to perform "all the drudgery of man, while he is to look on in self-complacent ease." Without supposing that they would rid society of all misery, they would make life a lot easier for man. "Hence it is," he wrote, that Americans "look with unmixed delight at the triumphant march of Mechanism."[14]

Similarly, the German-born American John A. Etzler in his 1833 book, *The Paradise Within the Reach of All Men*, argued that the new machinery now made it possible for man to create a paradise "where anything desirable for human life may be had," where the individual may "lead a life of continual happiness, of enjoyments yet unknown; free himself from almost all the evils that afflict mankind, except death, and even put death far beyond the common period of human life, and finally render it less afflicting." He and others were optimistic that individuals could harness the energy of wind, water, and sun to channel the power of machinery in directions that would benefit the entire society.[15]

From the time of the Civil War to the end of World War II, the future-consciousness of Americans underwent a change. As the United States became a first-rate economic power, the successful entrepreneur Andrew Carnegie described the new forces and America's achievements in terms of a "triumphant democracy." As more and more people acknowledged the beneficent effects of the fusion of America's ideals with the twin energies of industrialization and electricity, nevertheless there were, as mentioned earlier, labor, racial, ethnic, and urban problems.

During this period, laissez-faire economic libertarianism

was the prevailing ideology of the United States until the early 1900s when government reforms were introduced at the national level. The laissez-faire ideology, which advocated no government or limited regulation of the economy, again temporarily prevailed in the 1920s. By the early 1930s there was a worldwide economic meltdown, the Great Depression, which nearly paralyzed the country and led to massive unemployment.

After World War II the United States entered a new phase in history. Some people referred to it as the "post-industrial period," one in which society was shaped largely by the impact of electronics, computers, and new forms of technology. Not unlike the earlier shift in the nineteenth century, from an agricultural-rural society to an industrial-urban setting, the new crossing to a post-industrial culture profoundly altered the spectrum of choices available to the individual. New technological changes made possible new methods of production, new products, and new services. Human energies formerly channeled into the production of goods were spent in service-oriented jobs and careers. As society advanced from an industrial to a highly technological society, new needs and desires were created, thus continually multiplying high expectations. Americans brought technology to a pitch of perfection that seventy years ago could not have been imagined. In the twenty-first century we live in a world largely defined by technology and globalization.[16]

POTENCY OF THE DREAM

Indeed, the crossing to a highly technological-metropolitan society has been profoundly influencing the lives of individuals and altering American institutions. We are entering a time in our history where we are experiencing a continuing revolution in time and space relationships as well as seeing the digitization, virtualization, and automation of more and more things. The new technologies have thrust a new scale of life upon us. While the American Dream has "staying power," as scholars on the Dream point out, how will it fare in our new setting? We should not want to romanticize it at the expense of not discussing real and divisive issues, such as the enormous disparity in income, limited availability of essential goods, services, and opportunities, and race and gender prejudice.[17]

Part of the American Dream is based on the idea that with work and determination every individual, regardless of background, has equal opportunity to achieve her or his aspirations, that America is a place where the individual can make it if he or she tries, where anything is possible. The nation was built on people's dreams and labors. While "making it" generally has meant rising in the social ladder and doing well financially, it is not the essence of the Dream. Consistent with the "one for all and all for one" concept, it's the dream for a freer, better, and fuller life for everyone. It evolved from the Founders' ideals and the hearts and souls of the millions of people who have built this nation.

As mentioned earlier, the Dream lured tens of millions of people from Europe. The nation was opened to new and increasingly diverse groups. In many ways the story of America is the story of ordinary individuals of different creed, race, gender, and class attempting to pursue their dreams and what happened when they tried to realize them. The pursuit of the American Dream is inseparable from our nation's creed of individual freedom, equality, justice, and opportunity for everyone. Though the Founding Fathers did not actually talk about the Dream, they would have understood it. Its essence reflects the Founders' ideals.

Inspired by the land of promise and opportunity, many individuals migrated to America to find work, to start a business, to raise a family. While we all know of individuals who, through hard work, accomplished much, we also know that not all individuals compete or participate on an equal playing field. For example, race and class inequalities are often related to family wealth. As Heather Johnson points out in her study, *The American Dream and the Power of Wealth*, family wealth frequently plays an important role in many people's good fortune and the attainment of their dreams.[18]

Of course, there's a difference between equality of opportunity for individuals to achieve their potential and that of equality of condition. While most people would not expect equality of condition, they want as much equality of opportunity as possible. As the Founding Fathers knew, America can never have one hundred percent equality, liberty, and fairness available to everyone. However, as James Madison put it so well, Americans "should strive toward the least imperfect society possible." Individuals committed to America's ideals should want to face issues to make it possible for as many individuals as possible to go after their dreams. In the spirit of "one for all and all for one," they should strive continuously to find a healthy balance between individualism and social responsibility, self-reliance, and government assistance.

Because the Dream is an exceptionally powerful concept, it is politically potent. During the past thirty years America's political parties have stayed in close touch with the concept, which does not belong to any one political party or group. It belongs to all Americans. "Giving people a chance to live their dreams," President William Clinton said in his last State of the Union Address in 2000, "is not a Democratic or a Republican issue, . . . [it] is an American issue."[19]

Throughout the history of the United States, from the time of George Washington to Donald Trump, America's political leaders and parties have differed on ideologies and policies. In the formative years of the new nation, two contradictory visions predominated. On the one hand, Jefferson, who believed freedom meant individual autonomy and independence, put human rights and individual self-development at the core of the American promise. On the other, Alexander Hamilton, America's first secretary of the treasury, thought that a stronger and more vigorous national government was necessary to secure and maintain peace and prosperity for the individual and the nation at large. Thinking that government should set the rules for the marketplace, Hamilton favored the use of protective tariffs and bounties to protect and foster the rise of manufactures. He was convinced that businesses needed the aid and protection of government. However, because he did not want government to intrude unnecessarily, he argued there had to be regulations. Though these two broad views clashed, Jefferson, Hamilton, and their respective supporters fully endorsed the ideals embodied in the Declaration of Independence and in the Bill of Rights.[20]

The first president to use the phrase "American Dream" was Richard Nixon. In the second year of his presidency in 1970 he argued that the Dream could be fulfilled "only when each person has a fair chance to fulfill his own dreams." President Reagan and some of his successors, Republicans and Democrats alike, made even more frequent references to the Dream. "There are no limits to growth and human progress," Reagan said in his Inaugural Address in 1985, "when men and women are free to follow their dreams."[21]

Notwithstanding ideological and policy differences between

the two parties over the years, they remained faithful to the concept of the Dream. Whereas Franklin Delano Roosevelt thought during the Great Depression that government "could right the wrongs of the free market and renew the American Dream for average Americans," Reagan—almost half a century later—consistently argued that government at times impeded the American Dream and therefore did his best to scale it back. Believing that government was the problem, he thought its size "had to be reduced for the sake of individual self-improvement."[22]

A decade later President Clinton modified Reagan's analysis. "Government," he argued, "is not the problem, and government is not the solution. We—the American people—are the solution. Our Founders understood that well and gave us a democracy strong enough to endure for centuries, flexible enough to face our common challenges and advance our common dreams in each new day." Notwithstanding the differences in their ideology and policies, American Presidents talked about the American Dream and emphasized the importance of freedom, personal autonomy, individual opportunity, free enterprise, and individual fulfillment. Though Democrats, Republicans, and Independents in general disagree on many things, they grant each other the right to dream.[23]

In his 1997 State of the Union Address, President Clinton declared, "America is far more than a place. It is an idea." He hoped to "make the American dream of opportunity a reality for all Americans who are willing to work for it. . . . We know big Government does not have all the answers," he continued. "We know there's not a program for every problem. We . . . have to give the American people . . . a smaller, less bureaucratic Government that lives within its means. But we cannot go back to the time when our citizens were left to fend for themselves. Instead," he continued, "we must go forward as one America, one nation working together to meet the challenges we face together. Self-reliance and teamwork are not opposing virtues; we must have both." He clearly affirmed the concept "one for all and all for one." "Our goal," Clinton argued, "must be to enable all our people to make the most of their own lives, with stronger families, more educational opportunity, and economic security."[24]

Indeed, the pursuit of the Dream is at the core of what this country is essentially about. Significantly, it has bound people together who do not necessarily have much in common in terms of status. It helped build a more cohesive American experience. While the concept of the American Dream is a sort of glue it should not detract us from the real issues in society. As mentioned earlier, in every generation there were cracks in the Dream. There have always been individuals omitted. Individuals committed to the concept of the American Dream should want to face real issues so to make it possible for as many individuals as possible to go after their dreams.

As Martin Luther King, Jr., pointed out in his letter from Birmingham jail in 1963, "[h]uman progress never rolls in on wheels of inevitability; it comes through the tireless efforts of [everyone]." If America fails to revitalize the American Dream it may mean, as James Truslow Adams put it, "the failure of self-government, the failure of the common man to rise to full stature, the failure of all that the American Dream has held of hope and promise."[25]

Indeed, the American Dream is rooted deeply in the American consciousness. It's a precious inheritance. For it to have even more substance, it should be embodied in the lives of more and more people. Intended to be all-inclusive and not the privilege of a few, we want all Americans, in the words of James Truslow Adams, to "dare to dream, . . . to grow into something bigger and finer." Our present situation calls for a renewal of commitment to the American Dream, making it possible for every child and adult to have an opportunity of living up to their potential. In their wisdom the Founders believed education was one very important vehicle for individuals to better themselves.

Fundamentally, the American Dream is about hope, the hope that every individual of whatever status has the chance to be all that he or she can be. It is inextricably connected to America's ideals of freedom, equality, justice, and opportunity for every citizen. In his "I Have a Dream" speech in 1963, Martin Luther King, Jr. reminded his audience that when "the architects of our republic wrote the magnificent words of the Constitution and the Declaration of Independence, they were signing a promissory note to which every American was to fall heir. This note was a promise that all men . . . would be guaranteed the unalienable rights of life, liberty, and the pursuit of happiness."[26]

Grounded in the Declaration of Independence, America's ideals lose not only their luster but, more tellingly, their meaning without the Dream. Every generation needs a spirit of hope and the American Dream has inspired the imagination of generations of Americans. It is part of our soul. Without it, America would see its vitality significantly weakened. Like our nation's ideals, the American Dream of a better and happier existence for everyone is timeless. America's development has been dominated by it. Because the Dream is part of our nation's lifeline, it is indispensable in sustaining America's identity and mission and safeguarding and energizing its ethos.

CHAPTER THREE
THE PURSUIT OF HAPPINESS:
A BASIC RIGHT

America was founded on a set of ideas. Its mission, "one for all and all for one," depends on the ideals of freedom, justice, equality, and the pursuit of happiness that are rooted in the Declaration of Independence. They are the core principles of American life. As previously discussed, since the drafting of the Declaration happiness has been a national goal. Pursuing it is an individual's basic right. The phrase "pursuit of happiness" treats happiness as a concrete and realizable goal. What is enshrined as part of each person's birthright is the right of the individual to design her or his own dream and to work toward it. As Howard Mumford Jones points out in his pioneer work, *The Pursuit of Happiness* (1953), each generation of Americans has taken the individual's right to pursue happiness as an accepted truth. It became central in American social and political thought.[1]

How do Americans pursue happiness? How do they pursue pleasure? Formulas to happiness and guides to pleasurable living have been available for a long time. Hundreds of books have been written on how to get more out of living. One of the earliest popular guides to living was Benjamin Franklin's list of moral strictures, which he regarded to be of "the utmost Importance to the Felicity of Life." Whereas John Adams, his Massachusetts counterpart, who engaged in "remorseless" self-scrutiny in his diary had urged individuals to "be just and good," Franklin put together a list of virtues. Believing that living a righteous life was an "art," he drew up thirteen virtues, among which were temperance, frugality, industry, sincerity, moderation, cleanliness, and chastity, to assist individuals in their everyday experiences. "Be in general virtuous," he wrote confidently, "and you will be happy."[2]

Successful as a printer, journalist, almanac maker, diplomat, and politician, Franklin has been acknowledged to be the first American to gain fame for having contributed to the common good. Inventor of the Franklin stove, the lightning rod, and bifocal lenses, among other instruments, he was the oldest and regarded as the wisest among the Founding Fathers. Upwardly mobile, he has been known by many as the prophet of American capitalism. However, money for the Pennsylvanian icon was a means to a greater end, namely public service.

Thomas Jefferson, thirty years Franklin's junior, asserted that "[h] appiness is the aim of life, [and] virtue," he argued, "is the foundation of happiness." Like his Pennsylvanian colleague, Jefferson was much revered. An eloquent promoter of virtue and education, Jefferson was, in the words of the nineteenth-century French historian, Alexis de Tocqueville, "the most powerful advocate democracy has ever had." A planter, lawyer, architect, surveyor, diplomat, and philologist, as he knew several languages, Jefferson was one of the most brilliant politicians in American history. When I taught, I enjoyed sharing with my students that memorable moment when President John F. Kennedy was entertaining the Nobel Laureates at the White House in April 1962. He said with a grin that they were "probably the greatest concentration of talent and genius in this house except for perhaps those times when Thomas Jefferson ate alone."[3]

In the 1760s, the Boston clergyman Andrew Eliot also declared in one of his more eloquent sermons that virtue tends "to promote public happiness. People," he argued, "are generally capable of knowing when they are well used. Public happiness is easily felt." In his judgment, individuals "cannot but perceive when they enjoy their rights and privileges; when they sit at quiet under their own vines and fig trees, and there is none to make them afraid; when the laws of the land have their course, and justice is impartially administered; when no unreasonable burthens are laid upon them." His Massachusetts counterpart and lawyer, James Otis, in his widely read "The Rights of the British Colonies Asserted and Proved" (1763), argued that the end of government is "to provide for the security, the quiet, the happy enjoyment of life, liberty, and property."[4]

During and following the Revolutionary War, American political theorists carefully considered the form of government that would work best for the people and insure them the pursuit of happiness. In his *Thoughts on Government*, published in January 1776, John Adams urged his colleagues to consider first what should be regarded as the purpose of government. "Upon this point," he wrote, "all speculative politicians will agree that the happiness of society is the end of government." Thus, he inferred, from "this principle it will follow that the form of government which communicates ease, comfort, security, or, in one word, happiness, to the greatest number of persons, and in the greatest degree, is the best." That, in the Founding Founders' opinion, is what constitutes a healthy and happy society, namely "one for all and all for one."[5]

To the Founders, then, and to many of their contemporaries the pursuit of happiness was essential. As the contemporary historian Darrin McMahon points out in his excellent study on *Happiness: A History* (2006), Adam Smith, the Scottish economist, philosopher, and father of capitalism, believed that true happiness lay in "tranquility and enjoyment," which had less to do with an individual's economic status than it did with the moral qualities of the men and women who lived in society.[6]

As previously discussed, an individual's dream for a

happier and more enriched and fuller life is at the core of the American promise. Everyone should have a shot at it. Americans should not want equality of opportunity to be regarded as simply a well-intentioned phrase. A challenge in American life has always been how to reconcile the rights of the individual with the larger social good. As one may hope that there can be a greater convergence between individuals' self-interest and the interests of society at large, "one for all and all for one," there always will be tension between individualism and social responsibility. That is a tension that will never be resolved fully. It is part of the human condition. Individuals pursue their own separate dreams and that is consistent with our nation's ethos.

Consistent with our Founding Fathers' intention, America should continually adjust to changing times and strive to make it possible for every child and adult to have an equal opportunity at living up to their potential, of growing, in James Truslow Adams's words, "into something bigger and finer." The Founders' ideals of life, liberty, and the pursuit of happiness, which are the mainsprings of our being as a nation, helped animate the American Dream. The right to "life" implies the right to dream of a healthy and full life. The right to "liberty" makes it possible for individuals to chart their own paths. The right to pursue "happiness" affirms the right to pursue your dream.[7]

However, what constitutes true happiness? To be sure, what brings happiness to some people may not necessarily work or be right for everyone. Its pursuit, as Adam Smith argued, is not simply the acquisition of things or pleasurable items. Happiness exists within us. Sometimes it is attained by simply appreciating what one has. While sensory pleasures can bring happiness, but are usually short-lived, happiness through love and compassion is usually more lasting.

Indeed, happiness is a great emotion. It often depends on the inestimable value of good health and good fortune. In terms of good health, in early 2013 a report from the Institute of Medicine and the National Research Council showed that Americans live sicker and die younger than people in other wealthy countries. It pointed out that Americans "have a long-standing pattern of poorer health that is strikingly consistent and pervasive" over a person's lifetime. The United States ranked at or near the bottom in several key areas of health: low birth weight; injuries and homicides; drug-related deaths; obesity and diabetes; heart disease; chronic lung disease; and general disability. Americans' quality and value of life have long been of interest and great concern.[8]

In the mid-nineteenth century, Frederick Douglass was concerned over the quality of life and the moral state of the country. Though in his 1859 essay, "Contradictions in American Civilization," he appreciated America's physical progress, the former slave was concerned that the country's moral development, especially the enslavement of people, did not match its material achievements. "The pride of the American people, the thing which they most frequently cite as a proof of their superiority over other nations, is the high degree of civilization which they have attained. . . . Unfortunately," he argued, "American civilization abounds in strange and puzzling contradictions," especially disrespect for human life. "One of the first features which mark the distinction between a civilized, and a rude nation," Douglass continued, "is the value attached to human life, and the protection given it by the former. . . . Respect for human life, and vigilant protection of it, is a feature of civilization absent in this country. . . . The same . . . is found," he continued, "concerning the protection of health."[9]

Twenty years later, the social critic Henry George in his classic text *Progress and Poverty* also marveled at America's material and industrial progress. He wondered the following: Could Benjamin Franklin in the 1770s have seen "in a vision of the future, the steamship taking the place of the sailing vessel, the railroad of the wagon; . . . could he have heard the throb of the engines that in obedience to human will . . . exert a power greater than that of all the men and all the beasts of burden combined, . . . what would he have inferred as to the social condition of mankind?" Plainly, thought George, Franklin "would have beheld these new forces elevating society from its very foundations, lifting the very poorest above the possibility of want, exempting the very lowest from anxiety for the material needs of life."[10]

Indeed, Franklin may have beheld as much. In a letter to the British politician, Benjamin Vaughn, he pointed out that it "has been computed by some Political Arithmetician, that, if every Man and Woman would work for four Hours each Day on something useful, that Labour would produce sufficient to procure all the Necessaries and Comforts of Life, Want and Misery would be banished out of the World, and the rest of the 24 hours might be Leisure and Pleasure."[11]

Similarly, the internationally renowned economist John Maynard Keynes in his 1930 essay "Economic Possibilities for our Grandchildren" applauded America's technological development. On the eve of the Great Depression, Keynes argued that the latest technological progress made possible significant increase in the output of goods per hour worked, individuals would have to work less and less to satisfy their needs. Thus, Keynes wrote, "for the first time since his creation man will be faced with his . . . permanent problem – how to use his freedom from pressing economic cares, how to occupy the leisure, which science and compound interest will have won for him, to live wisely and agreeably and well." He thought this condition might be reached by the year 2030.[12]

But let us, in 2019, suppose even further than did Keynes and Henry George. Could Franklin have seen, in a vision of the future, America's venture into space, communications by satellite, the harnessing of nuclear energy, the newest technical, scientific, and medical advances, what would he have inferred as to the social condition and quality of life of Americans? Would he have envisioned an America in which individuals share fairly the benefits and responsibilities of community life? Perhaps he would do so with qualification. As a Founding Father, Franklin was very much aware of man's basic appetites for power, fame, and money. Unless America abides by a system of laws, "men will never cease," he wrote to Joseph Priestly in 1780, "to be wolves to one another."[13]

To be sure, to live true to America's ideals, individual self-interest and self-reliance should exist side by side with the good of the whole. To attain happiness and make the American Dream come true for everyone, James Truslow Adams reminded us, "we must all work together." Not unlike the covenant Puritans laid out in Massachusetts in 1630, we should have "before our eyes our . . . community in the work, our community as members of the same body." It is "one for all and all for one."

CHAPTER FOUR
CONTEMPORARY THREATS TO
THE AMERICAN REPUBLIC

The United States is a great bastion of freedom. From the time of the American Revolution, America has been a defender of freedom, of democracy. When it became a world power after World War II, it became the leader of the free world. This chapter will focus on threats to the viability of the American republic, namely the deliberate manufacturing of lies, debunking of the free press and long-standing government institutions, corrosion of the rule of law, and racial and ethnic divisiveness.

Despite today's troubles on many fronts, nationally and globally, America's ideals are still the best hope for people everywhere. Notwithstanding existing authoritarian regimes like Russia, Iran, China, and North Korea, we are seeing many people around the world exercising the right of self-determination and seeking those inalienable rights that foster human dignity and progress. They want freedom from authority that has overstepped itself.

Over half a century ago, Americans had to defend freedom of the intellect against totalitarianism, more particularly Communism. Today, many defend freedom against untruths. In this information age, we have witnessed a fabrication of imaginary facts as well as a systematic and deliberate falsification of issues. With the founding of the internet in the 1990s, Google in 1998, Facebook in 2004, YouTube in 2005, and Instagram in 2011, and other forms of social media there is the instant and widespread capability to throw things out without facts. In some ways social media is the genie that we've let out of the bottle and cannot put back again.

Because in some sectors of society the pursuit of the truth is in disfavor, we should be alarmed by the falsification of facts. What is at issue is the right to report events truthfully. To maintain a healthy democratic society, we must affirm the Founding Fathers' ideals and insist on the accurate reporting of information. Motivated by a love for the truth, we need to care for accuracy, lucidity, and precision in our language.

In the formative years of the nation political leaders promoted free discussion and supported a free press. The American creed, as spelled out in the first amendment, stresses free speech and uninhibited, wide-ranging discussion. To the Founders, a free press was critically important for the viability of the republic. "Where the press is free and every man able to read," Thomas Jefferson argued, "all is safe. Our liberty depends on the freedom of the press, and that cannot be limited without being lost. . . . Were it left to me to decide whether we should have a government without newspapers, or newspapers without a government," he continued, "I should not hesitate a moment to prefer the latter." He sought to "preserve the freedom of the human mind."[1]

Approximately half-a-century later, Alexis de Tocqueville wrote in *Democracy in America* that the influence of the press "in America is immense. . . . Its eye is constantly open to detect the secret springs of political designs." While attacking on several occasions the independence of institutions, including the Federal Bureau of Investigation (FBI), Department of Justice, Judiciary, and the Central Intelligence Agency, President Donald J. Trump unfairly charged the free press of being "the enemy of the people" because of its reporting of unfavorable accounts pertaining to him. However, as every American historian knows, throughout our history the press has been an important safeguard to freedom of thought and expression. As Justice Hugo Black pointed out in the 1971 *New York Times Co. v. Sullivan* United States Supreme Court decision, in keeping with the Founding Fathers' ideals "the press was to serve the governed, not the governors." The press is to hold political servants accountable.[2]

The contemporary controversy over freedom of the press also has much to do with conscious dishonesty and organized lying, such as practiced by authoritarian governments. To them, history is not only often falsified, but also created. The perversion of history is commonplace. Though Hitler "can say that the Jews started a war," the renowned twentieth century British intellectual and novelist George Orwell wrote during World War II, it "was a lie." However, if Hitler had won the war it could very well have "become," Orwell argued, "official history" in Germany. To authoritarians, "a big lie [is] no worse than a little lie."[3]

Today Americans are living amid a fog of misinformation and lies, much of which is generated at the national level. In President Trump we have an individual who during the campaign for the Presidency as well as during his occupation of the Oval Office manufactured and continually relied on a bed of lies. His falsehoods are so widespread that many people, including school-age children, are aware of them. To be sure, historians find lies during any president's administration, but never at the excessive level Americans are witnessing today. At the end of his first year as president, *The Washington Post* reported that he had lied over 2,000 times, which averaged about 5 lies a day. Two years later over 8,000 lies had been documented. As acknowledged in several publications, it's an unarguable fact that President Trump has elevated lying to an unprecedented level. Moreover, it became a familiar feature of political life throughout the President's orbit.[4]

Presidential historians have long argued that the U.S. Presidency is a place of moral leadership. Traditionally, the president sets the tone for the nation. Surely, lying is not the right tone to set. Thomas Jefferson and his compatriots would be shocked by the volume and frequency of the lies in the Trump administration. "Honesty," Jefferson wrote, "is the first chapter in the book of wisdom." To the Founders, individuals need to stand for basic human values, especially honesty and integrity.[5]

This chapter is not intended to be a full analysis of Trump's presidency. Many books have already been written about the president and his administration, including David Frum's *Trumpocracy: The Corruption of the American Republic* (2018), Jon Meacham's *The Soul of America: The Battle for Our Better Angels* (2018), and Bob Woodward's *Fear: Trump in the White House* (2018). All too often the president has denied that he said or did things that are in fact clearly on the record. Sometimes "political language," Orwell observed, "is designed to make lies sound truthful . . . and to give an appearance of solidity to pure wind." Significantly, before his election Trump fanned the Birther hoax during Barack Obama's presidency, arguing that the president had been born in Kenya and was raised a Muslim. During the final year of Obama's presidency in 2016, about three-quarters of registered Republicans either believed that he was born in Kenya or were uncertain. Shortly before the end of his presidential campaign Trump admitted reluctantly that Obama was born in Hawaii.[6]

Some pundits and politicians, like former Democratic Governor Howard Dean of Vermont, have called the president a congenital liar. Gary Cohn, Trump's chief economic adviser in 2017 and 2018, told an associate that the president "is a professional liar." Many have labeled him a serial and compulsive liar. In some ways Trump personifies the concept "Doublethink," a term that Orwell alluded to in his novel 1984. According to Orwell, "Doublethink" gives one the power of holding simultaneously two contradictory beliefs in his mind while accepting them, such as when Trump said he did not know the newly appointed acting attorney general, Matthew Whitaker, when a month earlier he had said he did know him.[7]

Martin Luther King, Jr. in his famous American Dream talk in 1963 hoped that his four children would "one day live in a nation where they will not be judged by the color of their skin, but by the content of their character." While the issue of racism is still real and should be condemned, we have another demon, namely lying, which has to do with character. Though each generation of Americans has witnessed lies, hypocrisy, and deception, our generation is overwhelmed by them. They pose a threat to the essence of America's republic. They betray our nation's character. In no uncertain terms, our nation's values and character are in jeopardy. Individuals' strivings toward candor, freedom, and truth are part of the American promise. They should not be suppressed.[8]

Moreover, what surfaced during the presidential campaign was Trump caught years earlier on a hot telephone on the entertainment news television show "Access Hollywood" bragging in vulgar terms about kissing and groping women whenever he wanted to. "When you're a star," he said, "they let you do it." Many Americans, including Republican leaders, were outraged by his remarks. Trump's incivility, namely erratic behavior, lies, and harsh language, before and after his election, have scandalized many people. In addition, even some of his most loyal supporters have been uncomfortable with some of his tweets. We've witnessed behavior that we would not want our children to model. Trump's raging and bullying are common characteristics. However, like Texas Senator Ted Cruz, who Trump had belittled and spoke condescendingly of his wife during the campaign, many Republicans overcame any distaste they felt for Trump. They convinced themselves that a Hillary Clinton's presidency was unacceptable and that he would support their conservative agenda. During his first two years in the Oval Office, the president's behavior was emboldened by the unwillingness of Republicans, who controlled both houses of Congress, to perform their legislative oversight responsibility and keep the executive branch in check.[9]

During the campaign Trump also gambled that many Americans resented each other's differences more than they cherished their shared values. Capitalizing on the country's ethnic vulnerabilities, he used divisive language against immigrants, especially Muslims and Hispanics. His strategy was proven right, and he was elected President even though he received fewer popular votes than did his Democratic opponent. By capturing disenchanted voters in several historically Democratic Rust Belt states, Trump won in the Electoral College, 304-227.[10]

The cultural divisiveness that he helped foster continued during his administration. Some political and economic decisions deeply divided America along lines of race, national origin, and cultural identity. History has shown that racism, nativism, and isolationism are often driven by fears, and that an authoritarian attains his goals through the people by riding and manipulating those fears.

Though a study of America clearly shows that keeping its doors open to immigrants throughout much of its history has kept the nation energized and released fusion-like bursts of energy, President Trump insisted on building a wall along the southern border to keep out illegal immigrants as well as preventing refugees seeking asylum from entering the United States. An ugly consequence from the policies of his administration led to the unconscionable separation of immigrant families and the locking of children in cages.

When in August 2017 Ku Klux Klansmen (KKK) and neo-Nazis gathered in Charlottesville, Virginia, and clashed with anti-KKK and neo-Nazi protesters, Trump referred to it as a display of hatred, bigotry, and violence on both sides. That was "as if," historian Jon Meacham argues in *The Soul of America*, "there were more than one side of a conflict between neo-Nazis who idolized Adolf Hitler and Americans who stood against Ku Klux Klansmen and white nationalists." Neo-Nazi and KKK beliefs are totally antithetical to America's ideals. Prejudices cripple a nation, and Trump's policies and statements help exacerbate them. Polarization has become a kind of disease. Jefferson rightly noted in a letter to John Adams in 1816 that "[b]igotry is the disease of ignorance. . . . Education and free discussion are the antidotes."[11]

Throughout American history, blacks, immigrants, women, among others, have involved themselves in struggles for more individual freedom of expression as well as human rights. Half a century ago many youths identified themselves with social outcasts: the poor, blacks, women, migrant farm workers, and undernourished and underprivileged peoples. Having grown up believing in freedom and equality for every individual and in a government of, by, and for the people, those were principles that they affirmed and could live by.

Today, women, members of the LGBTQ community, and blacks have been profoundly awakened to human rights and harassment issues. In keeping with the Founding Fathers' ideals, they protested civil and human rights violations. "I hold it that a little rebellion now and then," Jefferson wrote in 1787, "is a good thing, and as necessary in the political world as storms in the physical." Unsuccessful protests "generally establish," he continued, "the encroachments on the rights of the people which have produced them. An observation of this truth should render honest republican governors . . . mild" in their response to them. "It is a medicine necessary for the sound health of government." In the spring 2017 the Me Too movement demonstrated against the widespread prevalence of sexual assault and harassment. A year later the "March for Our Lives" massive rallies urged lawmakers to address gun control issues. On June 30th thousands marched in "Families Belong Together" rallies. Those protests were electric moments.[12]

During the civil rights struggle in the 1960s, James Baldwin, the late renowned American novelist and social critic, wrote that to "be a Negro in this country and to be relatively conscious is to be in a rage almost all the time." What he observed then also applies today to women, LGBTQs, Hispanics, and other people of color. Building upon the women's movement in the 1960s, women are not only fighting sexual harassment but, as Alice Rossi, a pioneering feminist and sociologist wrote in 1964, for sex equality as well, for "a socially androgynous conception of the roles of men and women." As a result of the congressional election in 2018, in January 2019 there was a record one hundred and twenty-seven women members in the House of Representatives. Moreover, racial minorities, young people, and women in general appear to be the future of American politics.

Significantly, while there are many things that divide us, there are many more things that unite us. As the Dalai

Lama, renowned spiritual leader of the Tibetan people, points out in *Joy* (2016), "our common humanity, our human emotions, and our fundamental desire to be happy and avoid suffering" unite us. Instead of being divided against each other, Americans need to work together and care for one another. We are deeply connected. Everyone experiences fear, sadness, and disappointment. Everyone also experiences joy. Sometimes we can feel the glow of people. However, like earlier times in our history Americans will not agree on everything. People will not necessarily come down on the same side of economic, political, and social issues. Some Americans are liberal. Some are conservative. Some are moderate. As noted earlier, while affirming "one for all and all for one" Alexandre Dumas in *The Three Musketeers* reminded his readers that "united we stand, divided we fall."[13]

In *Trumpocracy*, David Frum, a Canadian and American political commentator and a senior editor of *The Atlantic*, argues that what is also "spreading today is repressive kleptocracy, led by rulers motivated by greed rather than by the deranged idealism of Hitler or Stalin or Mao." There is a poisonous enticement to greed. "Their goal," Frum continued, "is self-enrichment; the corrosion of the rule of law is the necessary means." In the history of the United States there has never before been so many presidential advisers and Cabinet members forced to resign, found guilty of crimes, or involved in scandals. At times it appears the White House is dysfunctional and that there's a paralysis of governance.[14]

In May 2017 Deputy Attorney General Rod Rosenstein appointed Robert Mueller, who had run the FBI for twelve years, as special counsel to investigate potential Russian meddling in the 2016 presidential election and any connection Russia might have had with the Trump campaign. Mueller was authorized to pursue any potential crime. At the time of this writing four former Trump advisers, twenty-seven Russian nationals, three Russian companies, one California man, and one London-based lawyer have been indicted. As George Washington rightfully observed: "Few men have virtue to withstand the highest bidder."[15]

The Founding generation warned of "the desire in foreign powers to gain an improper ascendant in our councils. How could they better gratify this than by raising a creature of their own to the chief magistracy of the Union." Frum pointed out that for "more than two centuries . . . those warnings were heeded. This time, not." In January 2019, *The New York Times* and *The Washington Post* confirmed that in May 2017 the FBI launched a counterintelligence inquiry into whether Trump was working for Russia shortly after the president fired FBI Director James B. Comey. The Mueller special counsel team continued the line of inquiry. It is shocking that for the first time in our history America's leading law enforcement agency investigated whether a sitting president was working with a foreign adversary.[16]

In late March 2019, the special counsel team submitted its report to Attorney General William P. Barr. It did not find evidence of conspiracy with Russia by the president and his aides during the campaign. However, the report did not exonerate Trump of possible obstruction of justice. Presidential historians remind us that the Founding Fathers believed that if there is any suspicion of wrongdoing by the president, Congress should investigate. As mentioned earlier, it is their oversight responsibility.

In some ways America has hit a low. Witnessing a conflict between high and low ethical standards, we cannot afford to be passive observers. Too much is at stake. The threats to the republic are too severe. In addition, individuals' ability to pursue happiness, to pursue their dream, is in jeopardy. The nagging question is whether we can ever strengthen America's high standards that we have seen weakened in recent times. The sense of urgency that Frederick Douglass highlighted in his "What to the Slave is the Fourth of July?" speech in 1862 applies here. "The feeling of the nation must be quickened," he argued; "the conscience of the nation must be roused. The propriety of the nation must be startled." Because for over two hundred years America has been resilient in the face of crises, surely today's issues can be addressed.[17]

.

CHAPTER FIVE
LIVING A FULFILLING LIFE

As Americans we are united by a set of lofty and admirable ideals and values. Today's social, economic, and political issues make a demand for a higher commitment to them. According to the former Secretary of State Condoleezza Rice in an interview on March 1, 2018, Americans have "lost sight" of the nation's ideals. "We're not as committed to some of the values [and] principles." Living at a time when many individuals have little income and security, experience race and gender prejudice, as well as suffering other injustices, to many Americans it appears that our society has lost its moral compass.[1]

Indeed, have we lost our central direction, our grand purpose? Is the nation's vitality diminishing? Are we suffering from infidelity to the Founders' ideals? Do we have a lowered motivation to do what is right? To be a vibrant community we must not lose our spark. For society to function effectively some measure of consensus must exist. No matter how fragmented our society might be, it must embrace its fundamental values and agree on certain truths. America needs to return to its center, to its values. The Founders' ideals should be continuously affirmed. They're to be treasured. Extending to everyone, we need to cultivate them and enlarge the human spirit.

"America," the late novelist F. Scott Fitzgerald reminded his generation three quarters of a century ago, "is a willingness of the heart." Today's social issues should be addressed not merely by the intellect, but by the heart as well. If America slumbers, it is not because of a lack of means but because of a failure of heart and spirit. What can each one of us put our heart into? We should fuse our nation's ideals with the human spirit, both individually and collectively. "One for all and all for one," which reflects America's promise, is a moral standard that we should strive to fulfill.

Not unlike many times in the past, we can address current threats to the republic and recover from today's malaise. In the wake of turbulent times, such as during the Civil War, Great Depression, and the 1960s, America had the capacity for self-renewal. Each generation encountered a different reality and sought to bring new vitality to America's values. In the face of challenges, our nation's ideals can be revitalized for as long as the people affirm them. In every generation Americans did great things, and we must again.

The United States has undergone an enormous amount of change during its history. As mentioned earlier, for over two centuries Americans have debated the effects of social and economic changes on the lives of individuals. As a "dynamic society," the former psychologist Erik Erikson wrote in *Childhood and Society* in 1950, America subjects its citizens "to more extreme contrasts and abrupt changes during a lifetime . . . than is normally the case with other great nations." However, in this highly technological society, which has given us significant material advances, the pace of life and changes have become even more intense. It is not just quickening but also, in terms of communication, it's overwhelming. Life is far from equilibrium.[2]

Consequently, we need to be more attentive to how we lead our lives. As we assess our values and reflect upon our sense of direction, we should care about our character. Many people do not spend enough time and effort thinking about the meaning of life. It makes little sense for individuals to invest years of study and to work toward their dream but to spend little time caring about their character. While we engage in activities that we often do out of necessity, we especially need to do things that we care deeply about. We cannot hope to make society a better and happier place if we do not wish it for ourselves. While we all can't be excellent at everything we do, we should not have to settle for mediocrity. If something is worth doing, it's worth doing well.

To be sure, when we're free to make up our own mind and our own decisions, the better off we are to be our true selves. However, how many individuals spend much time doing things that, upon examination, are simply not worth doing? What activities intrude into our quality of life? Can we get rid of any of them? We should say "No" to some activities so that we fully enjoy the ones we engage in. As Benjamin Franklin argued in *Poor Richard's Almanac* (1739), "wish not so much to live long as to live well." What are those things we would like to continue or change? What is it we do that we would like to explore further in the future? While choosing our direction with care, we should always allow room for growth.

Sometimes to grow, a person needs to change what he or she customarily does. How do we bring change into line with our purpose? All too often we develop set ways of doing things. However, to be fully alert, habits should not control us. While some of them may prove beneficial and inspiring, such as setting aside time each day for yourself, some may inhibit us, frustrating opportunities for self-development. Sometimes we may be too fixed in our ways. Just a minor change in one's routine can prove refreshing. Moreover, being spontaneous can lead to renewal and growth.

As we continually assess how we lead our lives, do America's ideals and values run deep in us? They are a great resource. We have good reason to be passionate about them. They are a cause for celebration. However, are we faithful to them? Each one of us should not simply live at random but be concerned over the quality of our own life. In keeping with the concept "one for all and all for one" and caring about how we live, we need to find ways to help others enjoy life. We all can help lift individuals up, make them feel good about themselves. We all have something of value to offer; we all can make a difference, such as volunteering and working in the non-profit world. While donating money to charities is commendable, so is bringing joy to people.

As the ingenious amusement promoter Phineas T. Barnum pointed out about a century and a half ago, the greatest "art is that of making others happy." Like on an airline, however, in the event of an emergency we should put on our air mask first because we can't assist someone else if we're not secure ourselves. We need to take care of ourselves without being self-centered. To live true to the concept "one for all and all for one," each one of us in our personal lives must be faithful to America's ideals and care about our character, blending individualism with social responsibility.

To be sure, it's important to remember that we're all interlocked with other human beings. As mentioned earlier, everyone experiences heartbreak, disappointment, and sadness. We all need to learn to cope with the reality of the human condition, the joy and agony of life. Everywhere in the world there are people in need. Societies are often traumatized by poverty, deprivation, and violence. Notwithstanding innovations of the past two decades and the fact that our material world is continually improving, millions of people in the United States do not have adequate food and housing. As President Franklin D. Roosevelt argued during the Depression, "the test of our progress is not whether we add more to the abundance of those who have much: it is whether we provide enough for those who have too little."

The realization that we're all connected helps us become more empathetic and compassionate. As Thomas Jefferson urged his colleagues, "lose no occasion of exercising your dispositions to be . . . generous, to be charitable, to be humane, to be true. . . . Consider every act of this kind as an exercise which will strengthen your moral faculties and increase your worth." How we respond to people's suffering and well-being can make a big difference in our lives. We all have opportunities to be kind and charitable. As the late John Gardner, renowned educator, former Secretary of Education, Health, and Welfare, and recipient of the Presidential Medal of Freedom, pointed out in *Self-Renewal: The Individual and the Innovative Society* (1965): "The joy and suffering of those we love are part of our own experience. We feel their triumphs and defeats, their hopes and fears, their anger and pity, and our lives are richer for it." To be sure, we should rejoice in someone else's accomplishments.[3]

Not being solitary individuals, there's also the realization that we've been helped by others. We all came into this world needing two people. We're not alone. By being "one for all and all for one," we are part of a caring community. Now and then we're to think about important relationships we have with family and friends. They are central in holding people together. As we cherish time we spend with them, we should also value and enjoy the profound beauty in nature, such as the serenity of flowing water, the majesty of trees and mountains, the sun shining on the blue waters of the sea, and smaller things like the jagged edges of a leaf.

There's beauty to be found virtually everywhere. Sometimes taking a secondary road instead of a highway can be rewarding. When walking, occasionally look above eye level and notice different things. Observe details, big and small. To the six foot two and a half inches tall Thomas Jefferson, walking as a form of exercise was also very important. Writing to his wife, Martha, in the spring of 1787, he pointed out that "you are not . . . to consider yourself as unemployed while taking exercise. That is necessary for your health, and health is the first of all objects." Moreover, "a strong body," he later wrote, "makes the mind strong." Fit, virile, and a habitual walker, he urged individuals to "habituate" themselves "to walk very far."[4]

Connections with others and nature are essential to living a fuller and richer life. Everything is interrelated, interdependent. According to most scientists in the world, severe ecological damage threatens life on our planet. We've witnessed alarming pollution of the air, land, and oceans with increasing quantities of debris that threaten the quality of life. We need to take care of the environment. Many Americans support the Green New Deal proposals aimed at addressing economic inequality and global warming. In addition, while caring for the environment and quality of life, we need to support efforts to modernize our infrastructure, namely roads, bridges, ports, airports, bandwidth, fiber-optic lines, and wireless networks.

To be sure, living life consistent with one's values and convictions is the most noble of human endeavors. Sometimes we need to take large, important actions out of deep convictions. As Jefferson put it so well, "in matters of style, swim with the current; [but] in matters of principle stand like a rock." Similarly, Ralph Waldo Emerson later noted in his famous essay "Self-Reliance," "nothing can bring you peace but yourself, nothing can bring you peace but the triumph of principles." Indeed, in terms of values, one should stay grounded, maintaining the clarity to stand confidently. We learn from experience that it's easier to make decisions when we know and act in accordance with our values. Above everything else, one's life, Emerson further noted, should be "for itself and not for a spectacle," preferring "that it . . . be of a lower strain, so it be genuine . . . than that it should be glittering and unsteady." Being "one for all" requires living a life that is personally fulfilling and consistent with America's values.[5]

Being ourselves as much as possible is also an essential step toward happiness. According to the Dalai Lama, the "ultimate source of happiness is within us. Not money, not power, not status. . . . Power and money," he argued, "fail to bring inner peace. Outward attainment will not bring real inner joyfulness. We must look inside." In this high-tech age we can become so hyperconnected with the outside world that we can become less connected with our inner self and values.[6]

VALUE OF A LIBERAL EDUCATION

The Founding Fathers and early educators argued forcefully that the viability of the republic and the manners and quality of life of its people depend greatly upon knowledge. While proposing that learning be generously encouraged, they argued for a liberal education that would enable individuals to develop their critical and moral faculties as fully as possible as well as inspire them to act as independent human beings.

Building upon our Founders' vision, America needs to continue to provide access to education to everyone. Education is not only an entitlement but a necessity. President Dwight Eisenhower said in his Farewell Address in 1961, echoing the sentiments of the Founders and most of his presidential colleagues, before and after his presidency, America must have "an alert and knowledgeable citizenry." To keep a society free, vital, and strong, we need educated and engaged citizens exercising their right and responsibility to vote, who in James Madison's judgment, would then elect individuals "of virtue and wisdom." Colleges and universities should continue to provide a liberal education, namely through unwavering support for the humanities, arts, and the sciences.[7]

Liberal education courses in the humanities, such as history, philosophy, and religion provide students with the opportunity to evaluate basic beliefs that guide human lives. Literature and the arts illustrate the depth and scope of human thoughts and feelings and the imaginative ways in which they are expressed. Social studies classes afford students an understanding of complex social and political institutions and an understanding of individual and social behavior. Lastly, the natural sciences offer them greater understanding of the nature and functions of man and the environment. Significantly, in their liberal studies students cultivate an acumen for distinctions, connections, argumentation, and verification. They learn that there is seldom a single explanation for anything. It usually is complex. Moreover, students are given the opportunity to organize and communicate their own thoughts and expressions.

Notwithstanding the value of a liberal education, in some places it's in disfavor. However, Malcolm Gladwell, English-born Canadian journalist and author, has argued that as institutions of higher learning and people flee from the liberal arts it leaves individuals "impoverished." A liberal education broadens and empowers people. As foreign policy analyst Fareed Zacharia points out *In Defense of a Liberal Education* (2015), it helps individuals "make a life. We all play many roles, professional and personal, in one lifetime." In this age of instant communication, information can be googled or binged in a matter of seconds. However, deep knowledge takes time and discipline to acquire.[8]

Associated with personal advancement, upward social mobility, and success, colleges also have the responsibility to prepare students to enter the job market. Young people, like their parents, grandparents, and others before them, generally want to make a living, create a home, and raise a family. In the process, however, and most importantly, faculty and students should continue to seek and value truth and follow the dictates of wisdom in their lives. While specializing in a field of study is highly recommended, the academy must continue to provide an environment in which the pursuit of excellence and the truth is fostered. That is an essential part of what the Founding Fathers meant by underscoring the need for an educated citizenry.

In the spirit of America's founding generation, a liberal

education implants in the minds of the people those elements that inspire them to use their moral and critical faculties as fully as possible. In 1796 in his prize-winning work *Remarks on Education*, Samuel Harrison Smith, a young newspaperman from Pennsylvania, provided a model sketch of the well-educated individual in the republic. "The citizen, enlightened," he wrote, "will be a free man in its truest sense, too well informed to be misled, too virtuous to be corrupted. . . . He will know his rights, and he will understand the rights of others; discerning the connection of his interest with the preservation of these rights, he will as firmly support those of his fellowmen as his own. . . . Immutable in his character, inflexible in his honesty," he continued, "he will feel the dignity of his nature and cheerfully obey the claims of duty."[9]

Through its *Ratio Studiorum*, the Society of Jesus's "Plan of Studies," Cincinnati's St. Xavier College at its founding placed a strong emphasis on a liberal education, more particularly on the humanities, the arts, and the sciences. Renowned for academic rigor and commitment to faith and justice, nearly two centuries later Xavier University continues to assert strongly its Jesuit ideals. As it prepares students for specific careers, its mission affirms the belief that the most valuable and practical education is one that prepares individuals for a satisfying and constructive life, that helps characterize them at their finest as human beings. In 2013 my son, Mike, a 1985 Xavier graduate and a corporate vice president at Microsoft, made a generous gift in my name to the University in support of the humanities. "I feel like the humanities can be overlooked in today's world," he said. The award is given each year to a "teacher-scholar who—in the judgment of students and peers—is excellent to outstanding in her or his teaching" in the humanities and "shows evidence of scholarship that is recognized by the scholarly community."[10]

In addition, a hallmark of Xavier pedagogy and spirituality is the phrase "*cura personalis*," namely "care for the person." Today's generation of faculty, administrators, trustees, and alumni rekindle the sentiments of St. Xavier College faculty in the early 1840s that the "culture of the heart and mind of youth constitutes the end of th[e] institution." The University fosters a climate that facilitates the development of the students' powers of intellectual, spiritual, and ethical discernment, and the connection of that discernment with action. One of the Jesuits' favorite texts in the nineteenth century was Cicero's "On Public Responsibility," which captured the College's civic intent. "We are not born for ourselves," the Roman statesman wrote over two thousand years ago. "We as human beings are born for the sake of other human beings, that we might be able mutually to help one another."[11]

During the past half century, Xavier and most institutions of higher learning have become more inclusive and attentive to diversity, including race, religion, gender, ethnicity, and class. By continuing to integrate ethics, religion, and social values, along with peace and justice and diversity issues in its studies, Xavier fosters a curriculum designed to liberate individuals, to enable them to become more self-aware, more self-governing, more understanding of the humanity of others, and more committed to the concept "one for all and all for one."

LIVING TO FULL CAPACITY

As individuals we are precious and possess capacities for learning, freedom, and love. Having potential for self-cultivation and creativity, we're to use our imagination to find new possibilities for ourselves, to keep refining and improving our lives. As we aspire to live a life of well-being, wisdom, and wonder, our journey is full of creative possibilities and, at times, there are inspirations that come to us from our conscience.

To be sure, there are certain things that are totally out of our control, things that we can't prevent, such as aging and death. While we can cultivate a healthy life style, illness affects all of us. As we age, the human body inevitably slows down. Nevertheless, one can still lead a life that is fulfilling by holding on to positive attitudes toward change, new ideas, and ventures. We need to keep the mind actively engaged. Moreover, we refine our thinking by inviting a wide range of ideas, by welcoming and reflecting on various points of view. Our window must be opened to new ideas as well as to new people who come into our lives. In addition, love and gratitude can expand our perspective on life.

Well-advised not to discount America's ideals and values, we should continue to have faith in our ability to construct a more humane society. In this age of enormous speed and unparalleled wealth, power, and knowledge, Americans possess the means to focus their efforts on goals that are more socially desirable. We have the capacity to enhance the quality of life for everyone. Because every American is part of the main, there should be greater convergence between individuals' self-interest and the interests of the community at large.

To live true to the motto "one for all and all for one,"

Albert Schweitzer, the late humanitarian, philosopher, and physician, reminds us that "[n]o one has the right to take for granted his own advantages over others in health, in talents, in ability, in success, in a happy childhood or congenial home environment. One must pay a price for all these boons. What one owes in return is a special responsibility for other lives." The Founding Fathers argued vehemently that individuals should act selflessly for the common good, having compassionate concern for everyone's well-being.[12]

Moreover, by serving and helping others we help ourselves. By becoming more empathetic, we become more empowered. In the process we make our own impressions, our own footprints. In our life's journey, it's not about how small or big is our venture, it's doing something that's ours and doing it well. While it is admirable to pursue a goal, sometimes you just let life unfold naturally, striving to live it fully and richly each day, each moment.

To be "in the moment" is to be aware, thoroughly alert, appreciating and relishing it. As we allow the wide horizon to come before us, we're more likely to get the most of our experiences and see more wonders. Sometimes we have an intuition, which is knowing or feeling something that helps us on our journey, especially when we're calm and relaxed. Every day might not be to our liking, but there's something to learn and experience every day.

By subjecting ourselves to different experiences, we develop the full ranges of our capacity for sensing, wondering, understanding, and loving. We are always becoming. Our whole world is a classroom. By staying curious, it potentially energizes us. Every moment is meaningful and invites us to engage. As we bring something to it, we often take something from it as well. We may not be able to decide or control what happens every day, but we have the means to decide how we respond.[13]

Significantly, living in the moment is very much about being free and independent. We need to be free to be ourselves, to live life with vitality and resilience. And when people act together, freedom is power. While each one of us has been shaped and influenced by our past and have a responsibility to consider future consequences, we live in the present. The past exists in our memories and the future in our plans. Though we learn from the past, we're to live for today and tomorrow. To be sure, it's about being realistic and positive, not being primarily preoccupied by mistakes or regrets of the past or delusional about expectations in the future.

Using well the time we have, we should pay acute attention to each moment, to each event. Moreover, valuing unique moments is a refreshing way to live. While relishing precious memories, we're to welcome new moments in our lives, such as feeling the magical spark of falling in love, seeing your child or grandchild for the first time, or experiencing extraordinary moments like the end of World War II when people forgot themselves and became part of the whole. These experiences, in turn, spawn new memories.

To cultivate the ability to be fully aware, one needs to be capable of being still, of sitting quietly, which by itself can be soothing. In our accelerated age, it's advisable to take short breaks for silent thought, settling down to minutes of quiet reflection. Silence can be a rewarding refuge. Perhaps each day we should set time aside for ourselves in a quiet place to cultivate an inner quietness. Our inner space is often where we can go to find peace, where we can meditate and relax. Nurturing oneself in that manner can be most satisfying and refreshing. I have personally found that a massage is a blissful opportunity to live fully in the moment.

To be sure, silence and meditation help foster serenity. However, for meditation to work well is contingent on one's level of concentration. We can practice being totally focused by choosing an object and focusing our mind on it. One may meditate while walking silently. When we feel the need to get grounded, we may choose to repeat mantra, such as "I am strength. I am peace. I am joy." Reading passages from scriptures or Romantic writers can also prove calming and inspirational.[14]

As much as possible, it is advisable to avoid being rushed. Given today's propensity of wanting to hurry things, it makes sense to take the time to think of things at great length, especially those things that we think are very important to us. In addition, we should avoid being rattled. Sometimes meditation, thinking of someone we love, or counting to ten helps us to be calm. What also helps foster and maintain calmness is reducing clutter around us, enjoying the feeling of open and unlimited airy space. In addition, at times too much noise can contribute to stress.

Most importantly, we're to savor life's blessings. On occasions, such as before going to sleep at night, it's helpful to reflect on them as well as recall some of the more meaningful experiences of the day. It's also beneficial in the morning to take a moment of quiet to review plans for the day, balancing personal priorities and responsibilities. While many of us wake up thinking about work, taking care of the family, participating in some activity, or paying the bills, we should, above everything else, be thankful that we have an opportunity to bring joy to whatever environment we're in.

Living in an abundant society like the United States individuals generally want leisure to grow. However, in our high-tech age can we enjoy leisure properly? According to Robert and Edward Skidelsky in *How Much Is Enough?*

(2012), leisure in the true sense of the word "is activity without extrinsic end." It is the "sculptor engrossed in cutting marble, the teacher intent on imparting a difficult idea, the musician struggling with a score, a scientist exploring the mysteries of space and time—such people," they wrote, "have no other aim than to do what they are doing well." It's feeling exulted after completing a challenging task. While passion is an igniting force, it's also about being enthusiastic in our activity. "Nothing great," Emerson observed, "was ever achieved without enthusiasm.[15]

While America's promise is inseparable from our nation's creed of individual freedom, equality, justice, and opportunity for everyone, it is also strongly associated with an individual's effort to succeed by his own initiative. In the nineteenth century it was commonly identified with the frontiersman, the lone individual moving west across the land. But also rich in the American past is the broad definition of America's promise in terms of what individuals might become were they able to act in accordance with their talents and feelings. Romantics like Emerson, Thoreau, and Whitman viewed an individual's success in terms of personal growth and fulfillment. They argued for more individual self-reliance. "Be a Columbus," Thoreau wrote in 1854, "to whole new continents and worlds within you, opening new channels, not of trade, but of thought." In *Song of Myself* (1855) Whitman wrote: "I am large, I contain multitudes. I exist as I am, that is enough. If no other in the world be aware, I sit content."[16]

America's increasing attention to technology and techniques of specialization heightened Thoreau's concern over the twin dangers facing the individual, namely wastage of intellectual power and dulling of the senses. He opted to live a life alone in the woods, away from the bustle of civilization. In his late twenties he built himself a simple cabin on the shore of Walden Pond near Concord, Massachusetts. Individuals, he thought, should inculcate the habit of knowing through their own senses, reflecting on their own and other people's experiences, understanding their own thoughts and opinions, and acting out their acquired wisdom and principles.

By placing the highest value on the individual, early American Romantics cautioned against a too-structured, too-mechanized, too-routinized society that leaves little room for the unexpected, for spontaneity. Subjecting oneself to a mechanized existence affects one's dignity. They encouraged individuals to lead lives that made sense to them. A century later, the philosopher Allen Wheelis wrote in *The Quest for Identity* (1958): "Identity is a coherent sense of self. It depends upon the awareness that one's endeavors and one's life make sense, that they are meaningful in the context in which life is lived."[17]

Wanting to live a fulfilling life, all of us aspire for the good things in life, namely health, fulfillment, friendship, love, and leisure. However, it's easy to fall into the trap of wanting 'more,' like money, success, and power. When is it enough? On the eve of the American Revolution, the Pennsylvanian John Dickinson, writing to Thomas McKean, a good friend and political colleague, pointed out that "moderation in everything is a source of happiness." Too much of anything can "throw us from the balance of real pleasure."[18]

In one of Benjamin Franklin's many letters, and he wrote several thousand letters in his lifetime, he shared a valuable life lesson. "When I was a child of seven years old," he wrote, "my friends, on a holiday, filled my pocket with coppers. I went directly to a shop, where they sold toys for children; and, being charmed with the sound of a whistle, that I met by the way in the hands of another boy, I voluntarily . . .

gave all my money for one. I then came home, and went whistling all over the house, much pleased with my whistle, but disturbing all the family. My brothers, and sisters, and cousins, understanding the bargain I had made, told me I had given four times as much for it as it was worth; put me in mind what good things I might have bought with the rest of the money." That was an instructive lesson for young Benjamin. Afterwards, when he was tempted to buy some unnecessary thing, he said to himself: "Don't give too much for the whistle." When he saw one "too ambitious of court favor, sacrificing his time, . . . his repose, his liberty, his virtue, and perhaps his friends, to attain it," he said to himself, "this man gives too much for his whistle." As Thoreau aptly argued, the "cost of a thing is the amount of . . . life which is required to be exchanged for it." Consistent with their admonition, no one, for example, caught in the whirlwind of success, truly wants that success to be at the expense of spending quality time with family and loved ones.[19]

Since the nation's birth Americans have dreamt of liberty, equality, opportunity, and happiness. An essential part of the American promise is individuals striving to attain what is the best and highest in them. Each person has human worth. No one should be made to feel insignificant. Achievement should not be confused with human worth. Each one of us should aspire to grow to our potential. We're meant to flourish. We should ask ourselves are we living to full capacity? What fills us up? How do we expand ourselves? As Aristotle thoughtfully noted, "knowing yourself is the beginning of all wisdom." While acknowledging our limitations, we should take pleasure in our talent. As we come to terms with our personal skills, talents, and resources, we should carry them out to the best of our ability. As the French philosopher and novelist Jean-Paul Sartre noted in his autobiography, "born of future expectation, [we] leap ahead luminously in [our] entirety."

Questions regarding the condition of the American people should no longer be phrased in terms of what we can do, but in terms of what we choose to do and what is desirable for everyone. As John Adams said it so well, "the happiness of society is the end of government." Moreover, he rightly argued, people know when they're happy, when society facilitates "ease, comfort, security, or, in one word, happiness, . . . to the greatest number of persons, and in the greatest degree." "One for all and all for one" must be willed. We need to reconnect fully with those values and principles that made the American promise so compelling to so many generations of Americans.

CONCLUSION

The United States has come a long way since its beginning, growing from small cities, towns, and farms to the largest economy in the world. Throughout its history Americans latched on to the nation's ideals. They identified themselves with their heritage, which encourages refinement of those qualities that characterize individuals at their best. As gardens bear the same flowers anew year after year, so in each generation the Founding Fathers' ideals must be born anew. We should be fueled by a passion to cherish and honor those ideals, fostering a strong sense of connection with them.

Tradition is a special element that holds people together. As Abraham Lincoln rightly argued, "the mystic chords of memory" tie generations of Americans together. By connecting with our roots, which echo in our collective memory, we foster a sense of relatedness, inspiring us to live true to the nation's values. In his Fourth of July Oration in New York in 1787, Robert Livingston, a member of the Committee of Five that drafted the Declaration of Independence, pointed out that "a precious deposit is given into our keeping; we hold in our hands the fate of future generations." Individually and collectively, we need to continually seed, plant, fertilize, flower, and harvest America's ideals in ever-changing circumstances to make it possible for every child and adult to have an opportunity of living up to their potential.

APPENDIX A

A NOTE TO STUDENTS: LAST CLASS, APRIL 2016

PERSONAL REFLECTIONS ON LIVING A PURPOSEFUL LIFE

As you pursue your studies, what is your overarching goal in life? What is your dream? Surely, it should be more than owning a house, attaining fame, or securing a well-paying job. In my judgment, President Ronald Reagan aptly defined the American Dream in his 1986 State of the Union Address. "The American dream," he said, "is a song of hope . . . that warms our hearts when the least among us aspire to the greatest things: [such as] to venture a daring enterprise; to unearth new beauty in music, literature, and art; to discover a new universe inside a tiny silicon chip or a single human cell." Reagan's definition is entirely in keeping with America's promise of the possibility of human fulfillment for everyone. Every individual has the right to live, to work, to be oneself, and to attain fulfillment. Each one of you has the right and expectation to become whatever your talent and your vision can potentially enable you to become.

Each one of you needs to define your goal, your dream, in a manner that is realistic and in keeping with your unique talents and personality. Pursuing your dream means choosing to live in ways that help you live more fully, more intensely, more consciously. It means seeking to live a life that is aligned with what truly matters and not one that is defined primarily by salary, wealth, or social status. It means living a life that encompasses all that you are and can become. And as you engage in noble work, you should dignify what you're engaged in by doing your best.

Because life is so precious, you should care about the architecture of your life. You should ask yourself, where are you heading? What is your destination? Which path may bear the happier and more fulfilling prospects? Is your direction in harmony with your basic needs and values? Is your life fulfilling? You should not merely drift.

Above all, one should live a life of purpose and meaning. Notwithstanding a person's age one should continually pursue higher development, live by one's values and principles. We need to be at the helm of our own life, be the master of our own destiny. Our life should be in line with our priorities. All too often, a significant event intrudes on a person's routine, such as the loss of a loved one or sickness. When that happens, one becomes more acutely aware of what truly matters. As a matter of course, one should—perhaps weekly—prioritize the things that are important to them.

In our digital age the world has grown exponentially bigger and invasive. New forms of technology can be convenient and helpful. There's an increasing dependency on technology. While inadvertently helping to accelerate the pace of life, technology has an impact on people's everyday lives, their health, and their relationships. Some individuals are inundated with distractions, overwhelmed by their ever-present smartphone and full email boxes. At times individuals walk texting and listening to music on their smartphones, often disconnected from people around them and from themselves. Digital devices amplify the busyness of people's lives. Thus, individuals should care about the relationship they have with technology. As much as possible, they should control it, and not vice versa.

In our fast age, individuals can also easily lose sight of

what is essential. They can overlook important local, national, and global matters, such as poverty, racism, and terrorism. Living in a rushed, harried, and stressful environment, they may sacrifice time, health, home, and happiness. In our high-tech society, it is increasingly harder to unplug and renew oneself.

At times individuals need to disconnect from their hyper-connected life and experience the feelings of awe and wonder—to experience something exhilarating and magical. One needs to take the time to admire the world around him. All too often, the sense of wonder slumbers within us. We're well-advised to awaken it in our life. Each one of us has the capacity to wonder, to experience something sublime.

When we feel the need to reconnect with ourselves, it is helpful to take a journey to some place special, somewhere meaningful, such as a place in nature with beautiful scenery. Green spaces often have a calming effect. While there, one should spend some time for quiet reflection.

On occasions we need to shut out the noise around us. We all need silent thought. The inner self is where one can find peace, and joy is when we're at peace with ourselves. We need to give ourselves time to relax, to ponder. It is sometimes helpful to sit somewhere quiet, close one's eyes, take deep breaths, and visualize, for example, the sunrise, the sunset. Be attentive to our inner landscape. We should not take it for granted, but to inculcate the habit of taking that moment of solitude and quiet, to investigate things inside and outside oneself. An effective way to reduce stress or to unwind is meditation, a massage, a good walk, or a relaxing bath. As you prioritize things, make quality relaxation a priority.

Moreover, and not surprisingly, silence in our society is

under attack from many quarters. Embrace the power of silence. We all need time away from the noise and the myriad distractions in society. For over two hundred years, hurry has been a cause of affliction in America. It has harmed many people. We live in a high-pressure world, and hurry is a consequence as well as contributor to it. American culture is obsessed with speed. Because of the contemporary poisonous attitude of hurrying things, Americans are often impatient with slow development. An important lesson I've learned is that it's often beneficial to slow things down and take the time to think things through. It also contributes to better health. Significantly, to minimize anxiety in our day-to-day life, expect gradual improvement, not instant gratification. You need clear thinking, realistic expectations, and a positive outlook. We need to be flexible and realistic.

In addition to the traditional stress of being over-busy or over-working, today there's also the stress of being deluged with social media information. You can be overloaded with information about the Kardashians and Beyoncé, among others, yet spend little or no time caring about the content of your character. You can be very connected with the world around you but lose connection with your inner self. Medical studies show that millions of individuals in our society suffer stress, sleep deprivation, or burnout, and that these high levels of stress can lead to greater instances of diabetes, heart disease, and obesity. Lack of sleep does not enable people to function at their best. Having adequate sleep enables you to fulfill better what you're passionate about. It is important to rest and relax, to reduce stress, and to focus more. Our nation generally focuses more on its Gross Domestic Product and economic growth than on the health of its people and the joy in their lives. A person is blessed if he is healthy and has energy.

In our day-to-day existence we must be prepared for the puzzles in life, especially the curve balls, and for all sorts of obstacles, challenges, and crises. As we encounter personal and social storms or are caught in a whirlwind of activities, we need to have a clear mind, cool head, and rise above the storms. In the process, we should prevent our emotions from snowballing. It's unproductive behavior to continually fret over problems. We should not allow worries and preoccupations interfere with what is truly important. We should not allow annoying outside influences to get the better of us.

While encountering these challenges, we should take a few deep breaths. Be calm. Reflect and put things into proper perspective. We have within us the ability to move from challenges to calmness. As our mind is calm, we should study disturbing elements and bring our will power to bear upon the matter. Calmness is one of the most precious qualities of human life. And as calmness becomes more and more a part of us, it gives us new strength as we encounter new challenges. It helps strengthen our resiliency. Calmness is also the pinnacle of self-control. It should pervade us. By cultivating it one acquires strength to live more fully. To have an ongoing presence of calmness, to be at peace with oneself, we must have a high standard of living that reflects the dignity of life.

In pursuing our dream, then, a goal should be to manage life with calm and confidence. In the process, we will have an impact on others. No one is without influence. We affect the lives of others. By merely living, we affect people. No one can make us nice or mean but ourselves. We may radiate sunshine and optimism on the one hand, or anger and pessimism on the other. We should ask ourselves, are we warm toward others? Approachable? Helpful?

In the end, then, fundamentally we should ask ourselves, what is success? What is happiness? As the American essayist, Winthrop Jordan, pointed out in his classic work, *The Majesty of Calmness* (1898), "[h]appiness consists . . . not of possessing, but of enjoying. It is the warm glow of a heart at peace with itself." Each one of us has the capacity to create our own happiness. It depends upon us. While many activities in our place of work as well as events in our community and in the world are out of our control, the quality of each day is up to each one of us. We should set out each day to make life happier for ourselves and for others. Most importantly, we need to take time to care for ourselves. We need to be wide-awake in our own personal life as well as fully present in the lives of others, especially those we love. We can be happier and move toward our dream through mindfulness of our well-being. Each one of us should empower himself to live an optimal life, to grow to fullest development as a person, to rise to full stature. We should periodically visit our inner self. When we do, we will more likely face the future with confidence.

APPENDIX B

BENJAMIN FRANKLIN'S PROJECT TOWARD SELF-IMPROVEMENT IN HIS AUTOBIOGRAPHY

I conceived the bold and arduous project of arriving at moral perfection. I wished to live without committing any fault at any time. . . . As I knew, or thought I knew, what was right and wrong, I did not see why I might not always do the one and avoid the other. But I soon found I had undertaken a task of more difficulty than I had imagined. While my care was employed in guarding against one fault, I was often surprised by another; habit took the advantage of inattention; inclination was sometimes too strong for reason. I concluded . . . that the mere speculative conviction that it was our interest to be completely virtuous, was not sufficient to prevent our slipping; and that the contrary habits must be broken, and good ones acquired and established. . . . For this purpose I therefore contrived the following method. . . .

I proposed to myself . . . thirteen names of virtues all that at that time occurred to me as necessary or desirable. . . .

1. Temperance. Eat not to dullness; drink not to elevation.

2. Silence. Speak not but what may benefit others or yourself; avoid trifling conversation.

3. Order. Let all your things have their places; let each part of your business have its time.

4. Resolution. Resolve to perform what you ought; perform without fail what you resolve.

5. Frugality. Make no expense but to do good to others or

yourself; i.e., waste nothing.

6. Industry. Lose no time; be always employed in something useful; cut off all unnecessary actions.

7. Sincerity. Use no hurtful deceit; think innocently and justly, and, if you speak, speak accordingly.

8. Justice. Wrong none by doing injuries, or omitting the benefits that are your duty.

9. Moderation. Avoid extremes; forbear resenting injuries so much as you think they deserve.

10. Cleanliness. Tolerate no uncleanliness in body, clothes, or habitation.

11. Tranquility. Be not disturbed at trifles or at accidents common or unavoidable.

12. Chastity. Rarely use venery but for health or offspring, never to dullness, weakness, or the injury of your own or another's peace or reputation.

13. Humility. Imitate Jesus and Socrates.

My intention being to acquire the habit of all these virtues. I judged it would be well not to distract my attention by attempting the whole at once, but to fix it on one of them at a time; and, when I should be master of that, then to proceed to another, and so on, till I should have gone through the thirteen. . . .

I made a little book, in which I allotted a page for each of the virtues. I ruled each page with red ink, so as to have seven columns, one for each day of the week, marking each column with a letter for the day. I crossed these columns with thirteen red lines, marking the beginning of each line with the first letter of one of the virtues, on which line, and in its proper column, I might mark, by a little black spot, every fault I found upon examination to have been committed respecting that virtue upon that day. . . .

I determined to give a week's strict attention to each of the virtues successively. Thus, in the first week, my great guard was to avoid the least offence against Temperance, leaving the other virtues to their ordinary chance, only marking every evening the faults of the day. Thus, if in the first week I could keep my first line, marked T, clear of spots, I supposed the habit of that virtue so much strengthened, and its opposite weakened, that I might venture extending my attention to include the next . . . . I could go through a course complete in thirteen weeks, and four courses in a year.

Appendix C

Excerpts of Founders' Writings

Benjamin Franklin's Letter to Samuel Johnson, August 23, 1750

. . . I think with you, that nothing is of more importance for the public weal, than to form and train up youth in wisdom and virtue. Wise and good men are, in my opinion, the strength of a state; much more so than riches or arms, which, under the management of ignorance and wickedness, often draw on destruction, instead of providing for the safety of the people. . . .

I think, also, that general virtue is more probably to be expected and obtained from the education of youth, than from the exhortation of adult persons; bad habits and vices of the mind being, like diseases of the body, more easily prevented than cured. I think, moreover, that talents for the education of youth are the gift of God.

John Adams's Dissertation on the Canon and the Feudal Law, February 1765

. . . Rulers are no more than attorneys, agents, and trustees, for the people; and if the cause, the interest and trust, is insidiously betrayed, or wantonly trifled away, the people have a right to revoke the authority that they themselves have deputed, and to constitute abler and better agents, attorneys, and trustees. And if the preservation of the means of knowledge among the lowest ranks is of more importance to the public than all the property of all the rich men in the country. It is even of more consequence to the rich themselves, and to their posterity. . . . Let us tenderly and kindly cherish, therefore, the means of knowledge. Let us dare to read, think, speak, and write. Let every order and degree among the people rouse their attention and animate their resolution.

JOHN ADAMS'S THOUGHTS ON GOVERNMENT, JANUARY, 1776

. . . Laws for the liberal education of youth, especially of the lower class of people, are so extremely wise and useful, that, to a humane and generous mind, no expense for this purpose would be thought extravagant. . . .

A constitution founded on these principles introduces knowledge among the people, and inspires them with a conscious dignity becoming freemen; a general emulation takes place, which causes good humor, sociability, good manners, and good morals to be general.

THOMAS JEFFERSON'S LETTER TO GEORGE WYTHE, AUGUST 13, 1786

. . . I think by far the most important bill in our whole code is that for the diffusion of knowledge among the people. No other sure foundation can be devised for the preservation of freedom, and happiness. If any body thinks that kings, nobles, or priests are good conservators of the public happiness, send them here. It is the best school in the universe to cure them of that folly. They will see here with their own eyes that these descriptions of men are an abandoned confederacy against the happiness of the mass of people. . . . Preach, my dear Sir, a crusade against ignorance; establish and improve the law for educating the common people. Let our Countrymen know that the people alone can protect us against these evils, and that the tax which will be paid to kings, priests and nobles who will rise among us if we leave the people in ignorance.

JAMES MADISON'S LETTER TO W. T. BARRY, AUGUST 4, 1822

. . . The rich man, when contributing to a permanent plan for the education of the poor, ought to reflect that he is providing for that of his own descendants; and the poor man who concurs in a provision for those who are not poor that at no distant day it may be enjoyed by descendants from himself. It does not require a long life to witness these vicissitudes of fortune. . . .

Throughout the civilized world, nations are courting the praise of fostering Science and the useful Arts, and opening their eyes to the principles and the blessings of Representative Government. The American people owe it to themselves, and to the cause of free Government, to prove by their establishments for the advancement and diffusion of Knowledge, that their political Institutions, which are attracting observation from every quarter, and are respected as Models, by the new-born States in our own Hemisphere, are as favorable to the intellectual and moral improvement of Man as they are conformable to his individual and social Rights. What spectacle can be more edifying or more seasonable, than that of Liberty & Learning, each leaning on the other for their mutual & surest support? . . .

Benjamin Franklin's Letter to Joseph Huey, Philadelphia, June 6, 1773

. . . For my own part, when I am employed in serving others, I do not look upon myself as conferring favors, but as paying debts. In my travels, and since my settlement, I have received much kindness from men, to whom I shall never have any opportunity of making the least direct return. And numberless mercies from God, who is infinitely above being benefited by our services. Those kindnesses from men, I can therefore only return on their fellow men; and I can only show my gratitude for these mercies from God, by a readiness to help his other children and my brethren. . . .

The [religious] faith you mention has doubtless its use in the world. I do not desire to see it diminished, nor would I endeavor to lessen it in any man. But I wish it were more productive of good works, than I have generally seen it: I mean **real** good works, works of kindness, charity, mercy, and public spirit; not holiday-keeping, sermon-reading or hearing; performing church ceremonies, or making long prayers, filled with flatteries and compliments. . . . The worship of God is a duty; the hearing and reading of sermons may be useful; but, if men rest in hearing and praying, as too many do, it is as if a tree should value itself on being watered and putting forth leaves, though it never produced any fruit.

John Adams's Thoughts on Government, January 1776

. . . We ought to consider what is the end of government, before we determine which is the best form. Upon this point all speculative politicians will agree that the happiness of society is the end of government, as all divines and moral philosophers will agree that the happiness of the individual is the end of man. From this principle it will follow that the form of government which communicates ease, comfort, security, or, in one word, happiness, to the greatest number of persons, and in the greatest degree, is the best.

All sober inquirers after truth, ancient and modern, pagan and Christian, have declared that the happiness of man, as well as his dignity, consists in virtue. . . .

THOMAS JEFFERSON'S LETTER TO PETER CARR, AUGUST 19, 1785

. . . Give up money, give up fame, give up science, give the earth itself and all it contains rather than do an immoral act. And never suppose that in any possible situation or under any circumstances that it is best for you to do a dishonorable thing however slightly so it may appear to you. Whenever you are to do a thing though it can never be known but to yourself, ask yourself how you would act were all the world looking at you and act accordingly. Encourage all your virtuous dispositions, and exercise them whenever an opportunity arises, being assured that they will gain strength by exercise as a limb of the body does, and that exercise will make them habitual. From the practice of the purest virtue you may be assured you will derive the most sublime comforts in every moment of life and in the moment of death.

If ever you find yourself environed with difficulties and perplexing circumstances, out of which you are at a loss how to extricate yourself, do what is right, and be assured that that will extricate you the best out of the worst situations. . . . Nothing is so mistaken as the supposition that a person is to extricate himself from a difficulty, by intrigue, by chicanery, by dissimulation, by trimming, by an untruth, by an injustice. This increases the difficulties tenfold. . . . It is of great importance to set a resolution, not to be shaken, never to tell an untruth. . . .

An honest heart being the first blessing, a knowing head is the second.

Thomas Jefferson's Letter to Thomas Law, Esq., June 13, 1814

. . . Self-love . . . is no part of morality. Indeed it is exactly its counterpart. It is the sole antagonist of virtue, leading us constantly by our propensities to self-gratification in violation of our moral duties to others. . . .

[G]ood acts give us pleasure, but how happens it that they give us pleasure? Because nature hath implanted in our breasts a love of others, a sense of duty to them, a moral instinct, in short, which prompts us irresistibly to feel and to succor their distresses. . . . The Creator would indeed have been a bungling artist, had he intended man for a social animal, without planting in his social dispositions. . .I sincerely, then, believe with you in the general existence of a moral instinct. I think it is the brightest gem with which the human character is studded, and the want of it as more degrading than the most hideous of the bodily deformities.

NOTES

FOREWORD

[1] Richard Hofstadter, *The American Political Tradition and the Men Who Made It* (New York: Knopf, 1948), 5.

[2] Danielle Allen, *Our Declaration: A reading of the Declaration of Independence in defense of equality* (New York: Norton, 2014), 275-2

[3] Lincoln's words are from the Lincoln-Douglas debates as quoted in Daniel Walker Howe, *The Political Culture of the American Whigs* (Chicago: University of Chicago Press, 1979), 291.

CHAPTER 1

[1] John Winthrop, "A Model of Christian Charity," April 8, 1630, Cambridge, Belknap Library, Harvard University.

[2] James Otis, "The Rights of British Colonies Asserted and Proved," 1763, Library of Congress.

[3] "Virginia Declaration of Rights," May 1776, Library of Congress.

[4] Roger A. Fortin, "Life, Liberty, and the Pursuit of Happiness" in William T. Alderson, ed., *American Issues: Understanding Who We Are* (Nashville: American Association for State and Local History, 1976), 138.

[5] Enos Hitchcock, July 4, 1788 Oration (Cambridge: Belknap Library, Harvard University).

[6] John Adams, "The Passion for Distinction," in Adrienne Koch, ed., *The American Enlightenment: The Shaping of the American Experiment and a Free Society* (New York: George Braziller Press, 1965), 268.

[7] John Adams to Thomas Brand-Hollis, April 5, 1788, in Koch, ed., *American Enlightenment*, 195.

[8] George Washington to Major General Robert Howe, August 17, 1779, Library of Congress.

[9] Thomas Jefferson to Peter Carr, August 10, 1787 in Koch, ed., *American Enlightenment*, 320.

[10] As quoted in David Frum, *Trumpocracy: The Corruption of the American Republic* (New York: Harper Collins, 2018), x.

[11] Darrin M. McMahon, *Happiness: A History* (New York: Grove Press, 2006), 321-323-325.

[12] James Madison to W. T. Barry, August 4, 1822 in Koch, ed., *American Enlightenment*, 467.

[13] Thomas Dawes, July 4, 1787 Oration (Cambridge: Belknap Library, Harvard University); David Daggett, July 4, 1787 Oration (Cambridge: Belknap Library, Harvard University).

[14] Noah Webster, "On the Education of Youth in America," 1788, Library of Congress.

[15] Simeon Baldwin, July 4, 1788 Oration, Belknap Library, Harvard University; Benjamin Rush, *A Plan for the Establishment of Public Schools: Thoughts Upon the Mode of Education Proper in a Republic*, 1786, Library of Congress.

[16] Thomas Jefferson to George Wythe, August 13, 1786 in Koch, ed., *American Enlightenment*, 312.

[17] Thomas Jefferson to John Adams, October 28, 1813 in Koch, ed., American Enlightenment, 356-357; Jim Cullen, *The American Dream: A Short History of an Idea that Shaped a Nation* (New York: Oxford University Press), 2003), 51, 66.

[18] Jon Meacham, *Thomas Jefferson: The Art of Power* (New York: Random House, 2013), 8.

CHAPTER 2

[1] Jim Cullen, *The American Dream: A Short History of an Idea That Shaped a Nation* (New York: Oxford University Press, 2003), 10; *Cincinnati Enquirer*, September 29, 2010.

[2] Walter Lippman, *Drift and Mastery: An Attempt to Diagnose the Current Unrest* (Wisconsin: The University of Wisconsin Press, 1914), 267.

[3] Herbert Croly, *The Promise of American Life* (New York: Macmillan,1909), 206, 400.

[4] James Truslow Adams, *The Epic of America* (Safety Harbor, Florida, Simon Publications, 2001), 31.

[5] Ibid., 31, 36-37, 68-69.

[6] Ibid., 174; Allan Nevins, *James Truslow Adams: Historian of the American Dream* (Urbana, Illinois: University of Illinois Press, 1970), 72.

[7] Adams, *Epic*, 174.

[8] Ibid., 135, 198, 404.

[9] Ibid., 325-326.

[10] Ibid., 411-412; Nevins, *Adams*, 72.

[11] Ronald Reagan, "State of the Union Address," 1986, Library of Congress.

[12] John McHale, *The Future of the Future* (New York: George Braziller Press, 1969), 3.

[13] James Madison to W. T. Barry, August 4, 1822, in Adrienne Koch, ed., *The American Enlightenment: The Shaping of the American Experiment and a Free Society* (New York: George Braziller Press, 1965), 466.

[14] Timothy Walker, "Defense of Mechanical Philosophy," *North American Review*, XXXIII (July, 1831), 129.

[15] As quoted in Thomas R. Harvey and Robert Disch, eds., *The Dying Generations* (New York: Dell Publishing Company, 1971), 66-67.

[16] See especially Zbigniew Brzezinski, *Between Two Ages: America's Role in the Technetronic Era* (New York: The Viking Press, 1970); Thomas Friedman, *The World is Flat* (New York: Farrar, Straus and Giroux, 2005).

[17] Sandra Hanson and John White, eds., *The American Dream in the 21st Century* (Philadelphia: Temple University Press, 2011), 2.

[18] Heather Beth Johnson, *The American Dream and the Power of Wealth* (New York: Routledge, Taylor, and Francis Group, 2006), 101-128.

[19] William Clinton, State of the Union Address, 2000, Library of Congress.

[20] Cal Jillson, *Pursuing the American Dream: Opportunity and Exclusion Over Four Centuries* (Lawrence, Kansas: University Press of Kansas, 2004), 70.

[21] Richard Nixon, State of the Union Address, 1970, Library of Congress.

[22] Michael C. Kimmage, "The Presidency and the Making of the American Dream" in Hanson and White, eds., *American Dream*, 33.

[23] William Clinton, Inaugural Address, 1997, Library of Congress; Cullen, *American Dream*, 25.

[24] William Clinton, State of the Union Address, 1996, Library of Congress.

[25] Martin Luther King, Jr., "Letter from a Birmingham Jail," August 1963, Library of Congress.

[26] Martin Luther King, Jr., "I Have a Dream Speech," August 28, 1963, Library of Congress.

CHAPTER 3

[1] Howard Mumford Jones, *The Pursuit of Happiness* (Ithaca, New York: Cornell University Press, 1953. An extensive examination of the origin and development of the phrase "pursuit of happiness."

[2] Louis P. Masur, ed., *The Autobiography of Benjamin Franklin with Related Documents* (Boston: Bedford/St. Martin's, 2003), 95-97.

[3] Jim Cullen, *The American Dream: A Short History of an Idea That Shaped a Nation* (New York: Oxford University Press, 2003), 64.

[4] William T. Alderson, ed., *American Issues: Understanding Who We Are* (Nashville: American Association for State and Local History, 1976), 138.

[5] John Adams, "Thoughts on Government" in Adrienne Koch, ed., *The American Enlightenment: The Shaping of the American Experiment and a Free Society* (New York: George Braziller Press, 1965), 246.

[6] Darrin M. McMahon, *Happiness: A History* (New York: Grove Press, 2006), 329-331.

[7] H. W. Brands, *American Dreams: The United States Since 1945* (New York: Penguin Books, 2011), 384.

[8] *USA Today*, January 9, 2013.

[9] Frederick Douglass, "Contradictions in American Civilization," 1859, Library of Congress.

[10] Henry George, *Progress and Poverty* (New York: Robert Schalkenbach Foundation, 1939), 3-4.

[11] Benjamin Franklin to Benjamin Vaughn, July 26, 1784, in Koch, ed., *American Enlightenment*, 102-103.

[12] As quoted in Robert Skidelsky and Edward Skidelsky, *How Much is Enough? Money and the Good Life* (New York: Other Press, 2012), 3-4.

[13] Benjamin Franklin to Joseph Priestley, February 8, 1780, in Koch, *American Enlightenment*, 91.

CHAPTER 4

[1] Thomas Jefferson to William Green Mumford, June 18, 1799, in Adrienne Koch, ed., *The American Enlightenment: The Shaping of the American Experiment and a Free Society* (New York: George Braziller Press, 1965), 339-341.

[2] Alexis de Tocqueville, *Democracy in America*, 1835 in Phillips Bradley, *Democracy in America* (New York; Vintage Books, 1945).

[3] George Orwell, "The Prevention of Literature" in Irving Howe, ed., *Orwell's Nineteen Eighty-Four: Text, Sources, Criticism* (New York: Harcourt Brace Jovanovich, Inc., 1982), 267.

[4] *The Washington Post*, December 20, 2018.

[5] Thomas Jefferson to Nathaniel Macon, January 12, 1819, Library of Congress.

[6] George Orwell, "Politics and the English Language," in Howe, ed., *Orwell's Nineteen Eighty-Four*, 259; David Frum, *Trumpocracy: The Corruption of the American Republic* (New York: Harper Collins, 2018), 6.

[7] Lionel Trilling, "Orwell on the Future" in Howe, ed., *Orwell's Nineteen Eighty-Four*, 296.; Bob Woodward, Fear: *Trump in the White House* (New York: Simon & Schuster, 2018), 208-9, 235.

[8] Martin Luther King, Jr., "I Have a Dream" Speech, August 28, 1963.

[9] Frum, *Trumpocracy*, 43.

[10] Ibid., xi.

[11] Jon Meacham, *The Soul of America: The Battle for Our Better Angels* (New York: Random House, 2018), 4; Thomas Jefferson to John Adams, August 1, 1816, Library of Congress.

[12] Thomas Jefferson to James Madison, January 30, 1787, in Koch, *American Enlightenment*, 314-315.

[13] Dalai Lama, Desmond Tutu, with Douglas Abrams, *The Book of Joy: Lasting Happiness in a Changing World* (New York: Penguin Random House, 2016), 320.

[14] Frum, *Trumpocracy*, 52.

[15] Woodward, *Fear*, 165.

[16] As quoted in Frum, *Trumpocracy*, 30; *The Washington Post*, January 14, 2019.

[17] Frederick Douglass, "What to the Slave is the Fourth July" speech, 1852, in David A. Hollinger and Charles Capper, eds., *The American Intellectual Tradition: A Source Book*, Vol. I (New York: Oxford University Press, 1993), 405.

CHAPTER 5

[1] Condoleezza Rice Interview, March 1, 2018, "The View," ABC television.

[2] See Erik H. Erikson, *Childhood and Society* (New York: W. W. Norton & Co., 1950).

[3] Thomas Jefferson to Peter Carr, August 10, 1787, in Adrienne Koch, ed., *The American Enlightenment: The Shaping of the American Experiment and a Free Society* (New York: George Braziller Press, 1965), 320; John W. Gardner, *Self-Renewal: The Individual and the Innovative Society* (New York: Harper & Row, 1965), 15-16.

[4] Jon Meacham, *The Soul of America: The Battle for Our Better Angels* (New York: Random House, 2018), xvii; see Jon Meacham, *Thomas Jefferson: The Art of Power* (New York: Random House Publishing Group, 2012).

[5] Ralph Waldo Emerson, "Self-Reliance," 1841, in David A. Hollinger and Charles Capper, eds., *The American Intellectual Tradition*, Vol. I (New York: Oxford University Press, 1993), 288-302.

[6] Dalai Lama, Desmond Tutu, with Douglas Abrams, *The Book of Joy: Lasting Happiness in a Changing World* (New York: Penguin Random House, 2016).

[7] Dwight Eisenhower, Farewell Address, 1961, Library of Congress.

[8] Fareed Zacharia, *In Defense of a Liberal Education* (New York: W. W. Norton & Company, 2015), 150-151.

[9] Samuel Harrison Smith, *Remarks on Education*, 1796, Library of Congress.

[10] Roger A. Fortin, *To See Great Wonders: A History of Xavier University, 1831-2006* (Scranton: University of Scranton Press, 2006), 23-25; John W. O'Malley, S.J., "Jesuit Schools and the Humanities Yesterday and Today," *Studies in the Spirituality of Jesuits*, Spring, 2015, 20-30.

[11] Fortin, *To See Great Wonders*, 27.

[12] See Albert Schweitzer, *The Teaching of Reverence for Life* (London, England: Peter Owen Publisher, 1966).

[13] Arianna Huffington, *Thrive: The Third Metric to Redefining Success and Creating a Life of Well-Being, Wisdom, and Wonder* (New York: Harmony Books, 2014), 165.

[14] Lama, *Joy*, 310.

[15] Robert Skidelsky and Edward Skidelsky, *How Much is Enough?: Money and the Good Life* (New York: Other Press, 2012), 9.

[16] Henry David Thoreau, "Walden" in Sherman Paul, ed., *Walden and Civil Disobedience* (Boston: Houghton Mifflin Company, 1960), 1- 227; Walt Whitman, "Song of Myself" (1856), Library of Congress; William T. Alderson, ed., *American Issues: Understanding Who We Are* (Nashville: American Association for State and Local History, 1976), 134.

[17] Allen Wheelis, *The Quest for Identity* (New York: W. W. Norton & Co., 1958), Chapter 1; Alderson, ed., *Understanding Who We Are*, 134.

[18] Skidelsky, *How Much is Enough?*, 13

[19] Benjamin Franklin to Madame Brillon, November 10, 1779, in Koch, ed., *American Enlightenment*, 90-91.

BIBLIOGRAPHY

Adams, James Truslow. *The Epic of America*. Safety Harbor, Florida: Simon Publications, 2001.

Alderson, William, T., ed. *American Issues: Understanding Who We Are*. Nashville, Tennessee, American Association for State and Local History, 1976.

Baldwin, Simeon. July 4, 1788, Oration. Cambridge: Belknap Library, Harvard University.

Bradley, Phillips. *Democracy in America*. New York: Vintage Books, 1945.

Brands, H. W. *American Dreams: The United States Since 1945*. New York: Penguin Books, 2011.

Brzezinski, Zbigniew. Between Two Ages: America's Role in the Technetronic Era. New York: The Viking Press, 1970.

Clinton, William. Inaugural Address, 1996, Library of Congress.

Clinton, William. State of the Union Address, 2000. Library of Congress.

Croly, Herbert. *The Promise of American Life*. New York, Macmillan, 1909.

Cullen, Jim. *The American Dream: A Short History of an Idea That Shaped a Nation*. New York: Oxford University Press, 2003.

Daggett, David. July 4, 1787, Oration. Cambridge: Belknap Library, Harvard University.

Dawes, Thomas. July 4, 1788, Oration. Cambridge: Belknap Library, Harvard University.

Eisenhower, Dwight. Farewell Address, 1961, Library of Congress.

Erikson, Eric H. *Childhood and Society*. New York: W. W. Norton & Co., 1950.

Fortin, Roger A. *To See Great Wonders: A History of Xavier University, 1831-2006*. Scranton: University of Scranton Press, 2006.

Friedman, Thomas. *The World is Flat*. New York: Farrar, Straus and Giroux, 2005.

Frum, David. *Trumpocracy: The Corruption of the American Republic*. New York: Harper Collins, 2018.

Gardner, John W. *Self-Renewal: The Individual and the Innovative Society.* New York: Harper & Row, 1965.

George, Henry. *Progress and Poverty.* New York: Robert Schalkenbach Foundation, 1939.

Hanson, Sandra and John White, eds. *The American Dream in the 21ˢᵗ Century.* Philadelphia: Temple University Press, 2011.

Harvey, Thomas R. and Robert Disch, eds. *The Dying Generations.* New York: Dell Publishing Company, 1971.

Hitchcock, Enos. July 4, 1788, Oration. Cambridge: Belknap Library, Harvard University.

Hollinger, David A. and Charles Capper, eds. *The American Intellectual Tradition: A Source Book*, Vol. I. New York: Oxford University Press, 1993.

Howe, Irving, ed. *Orwell's Nineteen Eighty-Four: Text, Sources, Criticism.* New York: Harcourt Brace Jovanovich, Inc., 1982.

Huffington, Arianna. *Thrive: The Third Metric to Redefining Success and Creating a Life of Well-Being, Wisdom, and Wonder.* New York: Harmony Books, 2014.

Jillson, Cal. *Pursuing the American Dream: Opportunity and Exclusion Over Four Centuries.* Lawrence, Kansas: University Press of Kansas, 2004.

Johnson, Heather Beth. *The American Dream and the Power of Wealth.* New York: Routledge, Taylor, and Francis Group, 2006.

Jones, Howard Mumford. *The Pursuit of Happiness.* Ithaca, New York: Cornell University Press, 1953.

King, Martin Luther, Jr. "I Have a Dream Speech," August 28, 1963, Library of Congress.

King, Martin Luther, Jr. "Letter from a Birmingham Jail," August 1963, Library of Congress.

Koch, Adrienne, ed. *The American Enlightenment: The Shaping of the American Experiment and a Free Society.* New York: George Braziller Press, 1965.

Lama, Dalai, Desmond Tutu, with Douglas Abrams. *The Book of Joy: Lasting Happiness in a Changing World.* New York: Penguin Random House, 2016).

Lasch, Christopher. *The Revolt of the Elites: and The Betrayal of Democracy*. New York: W. W. Norton, 1995.

Lippman, Walter. *Drift and Mastery: An Attempt to Diagnose the Current Unrest*. Wisconsin: The University of Wisconsin Press, 1914.

Livingston, Robert. July 4, 1787, Oration. Cambridge: Belknap Library, Harvard University Press.

McHale, John. *The Future of the Future*. New York: George Braziller Press, 1969.

McMahon, Darrin M. *Happiness: A History*. New York: Grove Press, 2006.

Masur, Louis P., ed. *The Autobiography of Benjamin Franklin with Related Documents*. Boston: Bedford/St. Martin's Press, 2003.

Meacham, Jon. *Thomas Jefferson: The Art of Power*. New York: Random House, 2013.

Meacham, Jon. *The Soul of America: The Battle for Our Better Angels*. New York: Random House, 2018.

Nevins, Allan. *James Truslow Adams: Historian of the American Dream*. Urbana, Illinois: University of Illinois Press, 1970.

Nixon, Richard. State of the Union Address, 1970, Library of Congress.

O'Malley, John W., S.J. "Jesuit Schools and the Humanities Yesterday and Today." *Studies in The Spirituality of Jesuits*, Spring 2015.

Otis, James. "The Rights of British Colonies Asserted and Proved," 1763, Library of Congress.

Reagan, Ronald. State of the Union Address, 1986, Library of Congress.

Rice, Condoleezza Interview, March 1, 2018. New York: The View.

Rush, Benjamin. *A Plan for the Establishment of Public Schools: Thoughts Upon the Mode of Education Proper in a Republic*, 1786, Library of Congress.

Schweitzer, Albert. *The Teaching of Reverence for Life*. London, England: Peter Owen Publisher, 1966.

Skidelsky, Robert and Edward Skidelsky. *How Much is Enough?: Money and the Good Life*. New York: Other Press, 2012).

Smith, Samuel Harrison. *Remarks on Education*, 1796, Library of Congress.

The Washington Post, December 20, 2018; January, 2019.

USA Today, January 9, 2013.

"Virginia Declaration of Rights," May 1776, Library of Congress.

Walker, Timothy. "Defense of Mechanical Philosophy," *North American Review*, XXXIII, July 1831.

Webster, Noah. "On the Education of Youth in America," 1788, Library of Congress.

Wheelis, Allen. *The Quest for Identity*. New York: W. W. Norton & Co., 1958.

Whitman, Walt. "Song of Myself," 1856, Library of Congress.

Winthrop, John. "A Model of Christian Charity." Cambridge: Belknap Library, Harvard University.

Woodward, Bob. *Fear: Trump in the White House*. New York: Simon & Schuster, 2018.

Zacharia, Fareed. *In Defense of a Liberal Education*. New York. W. W. Norton & Company, 2015.

Zander, Rosamund Stone and Benjamin Zander. *The Art of Possibility: Transforming Professional and Personal Life*. London. Penguin Books, 2000.